A WYOMING KID

Memoirs of growing up in the 40s and 50s

Don M Ricks

thebook@donricks.com

ISBN-13: 9798539636760
ISBN-10: 1477123456

Cover design by: Julie Morgan
Library of Congress Control Number: 2018675309
Printed in the United States of America

To Barbara, of course

And to the memory of Cody

And to each of those who carry the genes:
Beth, Jim, Kate, Margaret, Peter, Tanner,
Janna, Logan, Josephine, William, and Huxley.

CONTENTS

Remembering

In aerial photos from the time, Jackson, Wyoming, resembles a scattering of small farms. Some people live on an acre or two. Behind several homes a barn can be seen as well as an outhouse.

My earliest memory occurred in one of those barns when I was three or four. The details are hazy. I'm in the hay loft with an older girl. She seems five at least, maybe six. Other children seem to surround us, but I'm not sure. As an act of curiosity the girl may have messed with my clothing, though I'm not certain about that either.

But two memories from that day in that barn are vivid, one visual, the other tactile. I see an empty light socket on the wall. And I feel my first electric shock zapping through my right forefinger.

This book is a collection of memoirs. But it is not, as many memoirs are, an autobiography. I am a raconteur, a teller of stories. My first person accounts are *not the story of my life* but stories *from* my life.

A boy and young man growing up in small-town Wyoming seven decades ago could try out adult roles, could face challenges and risks now mostly withheld from the young. He could enjoy successes (and endure failures). If he was fated to grow up to be a raconteur, he could also collect good story material along the way.

The 85 short memoirs in this book recreate personal moments exactly as they happened sixty and seventy years ago, as nearly as remembrance permits. A few narratives have been smoothed with minor inventions, but every story is true.

People have wondered how, now in my mid-80s, I can recall my life as a child and youth in so much detail. It puzzles me too. I'm aware of huge blanks in my memory, long periods of total lack of recall. (I have trouble remembering where I put down that screwdriver five minutes ago too.) But story-worthy moments and events come back to me in flashes that encapsulate their entirely.

Photography provides a useful analogy perhaps. The photographer *sees*, amongst the clutter of visual images that life presents, the *pictures*, the images that reveal something to us, that freeze a moment of significance. She captures them with her camera. As a writer I *see the stories* in the passing parade of my old memories. The keyboard is my camera for capturing them.

Five Generations
In Wyoming

PHOTO. Five generations: My mom holding me on the left; Aunt Eleanor
holding my cousin Jim Ridgeway on the right.

1 *Two Kids, One Horse*

That summer on the farm my cousin Jim Ridgeway was 8. I was 9. We free ranged. We did stuff.

We chased a badger one day. Our exuberant young dog followed it headlong into its den. She came back out even faster.

We swam/waded/floated in the irrigation canal that ran below the house, each carrying a quart jar. Whoever caught the most frogs and water snakes was the winner. Our jars kept filling up. We'd pour out the squirming contents and start a new contest.

In the trees by the canal we picked out a young cottonwood five or six inches in diameter. Taking turns, we laboriously chopped it down with a hatchet just so we could yell "Timber" as it toppled.

After Sunday dinner at Grandma's Jim and I announced we'd walk back to the farm. We confirmed our intended route with the adults and took off. The first leg was a mile across Riverton. Then the hike continued six miles out into the country following what's now called Riverview Road.

Caught out in a thunderstorm, we ran back to the house. As I sat by the mud room door taking off my shoes, my eyes happened to focus on a steel stake protruding from the ground 30 feet away. Lightening struck it.

"We killed a skunk," Jim declared proudly. "But we didn't get any on us," I announced. "The hell you didn't," Aunt Eleanor said, grabbing a bar of Grandma's lye soap and marching us out to the well.

A pickup pulling a horse trailer came down the lane one day. A friend of the family had given us an old grey gelding, complete with bridle. As the horse backed down the ramp our world expanded. We were mobile. And we could steer.

Sometimes we agreed to let my cousin Carol, 5 or 6 then, tag along. Riding triple bareback, we all headed across the road and up into the hills. Our explorations brought us to a big irrigation canal. Curious whether the horse would swim, Jim reigned down the steep bank. The horse swam us across and lunged up the bank on the other side. Plop. Plop. Plop. One by one we slid over the horse's wet rump into the water.

Another time Jim and I came upon some cows and decided they needed rounding up. A heifer started running. The old cow pony, taking a break from babysitting, found his game again. In an instant we were on her tail. The cow broke left. The horse broke left. Jim and I—one behind the other, in sitting position—continued straight ahead.

We experienced responsibility as well as adventure.

As my aunt and uncle got in the car, Pete told Jim to start the tractor and move a pile of manure while they were away. Jim scooped up a heavy load, raised it as high as the hay lift would take it, then started driving. One tire rode up on a hump and the tractor gently tipped over, me hanging tightly onto the seat behind Jim.

Uncle Pete came home. He pondered the tractor lying on its side; the fully extended hydraulics; the big pile of spilled manure; and said nothing. Maybe he decided Jim needed no further instruction that day on the subjects of gravity and balance.

The words we most dreaded at breakfast were, "Time for you kids to clean out the chicken house." The chicken house was 40 feet long and 20 feet wide. It sheltered more than a hundred laying hens. The hens deposited eggs inside, and other organic matter.

Though Jim and I ranged widely, we had two tethers. One was an absolute prohibition against going anywhere near the river, which we obeyed absolutely. The other was Aunt Eleanor's piercing Yoohoo.

It carried half a mile. A single Yoohoo meant "Yoohoo too, so I can tell where you are." Two Yoohoos meant, in a good natured way, "Get your butts back to the house right now."

2 *Why Aunt Eleanor Shot the Goat*

A favorite ritual at family get-togethers was teasing Aunt Eleanor into telling us about the time she shot the goat.

This particular year we were gathered in a Forest Service campground near Pinedale, four generations with our various camping rigs. Billy Penton, an old friend from Lander, had dropped by.

Even the children knew the context of the goat story. It had happened many years before when Aunt Eleanor and Uncle Pete were farming just north of Lander. When a neighboring ranch family went on vacation, Pete and Eleanor agreed to tend their livestock and babysit their kids' pet kid.

The young goat was incorrigible. It raided the garden. It climbed on the vehicles. It wiggled its way into every structure on the ranch. And finally, it broke into the house.

Here's how Aunt Eleanor retold the story that day near Pinedale.

"I'd been in town shopping. When I carried my groceries to the back door, I saw a hole had been punched through the screen.

"I searched through the house. Every house plant had been nipped off at dirt level.

"Finally I got to our bedroom. The goat was standing in the middle of our bed. He looked me right in the eye, said 'baaaaa.' And crapped.

"I grabbed him by a leg, dragged him to the back door, and threw him outside. Then I grabbed the .22 by the door and shot him. Got him right between the eyes."

"But Mom," a cousin objected on cue, "You never shot a gun before in your life. And that was Dad's gun from the slaughterhouse. It didn't even have any sights."

"I don't care. I hit the little shit right between the eyes."

We laughed, enjoying the familiar, oft told tale. But

Billy Penton, our visitor, was quiet.

Then he chuckled, rubbed his chin, and said, "Me and my brother Bobby always wondered what happened to that damn goat."

3   *The Mouse Drowns, the Butter Survives*

My great grandmother, Ellen Simpson, finished churning and poured off the buttermilk. A drowned mouse splashed into the bowl. Today it's difficult to grasp how the event could have been a crisis, but for her it was. She didn't know what to do.

This would have occurred around 1910. By then the family, having escaped abject poverty in Denmark by emigrating, was settled in Cambria, a coal mining community eight miles north of Newcastle. The Cambria Fuel Company, intent on building a stable work force, treated its workers well. It had settled the family in a company house and paid my great grandfather good wages. They even milked their own cow.

But my great grandmother was poor because she believed she was poor. And she stayed poor until she died well into her 80s. After her death the family found her bureau drawers stuffed with brand new underwear, given regularly as Christmas and birthday gifts, that she had hoarded for years. The drawers also held the ragged underwear she wore every day.

The family recounted a story from when she lived in Sheridan with her youngest daughter and son in law. Her greatest pleasure . . . what got her out of bed in the summer . . . was her vegetable garden. She spent her mornings tending it and watered it lavishly.

Then she discovered the City mailed them a water bill each month. "We have to pay for water?" The bill was for only one dollar, and at a flat monthly rate to boot. But she would not be dissuaded. From then on she was seen walking between the rows each morning, bucket in one hand and dipper in the other, carefully watering each plant.

So we can understand why, in Cambria many years earlier, that dead mouse floating in the bowl of buttermilk posed an insoluble dilemma to the young wife and mother. She could not bear to throw out a perfectly good lump of butter; nor could she bear to sit at the table watching her children eat it, knowing the image of that mouse would come to mind.

She sought rescue. Those in the community who churned their own butter wrapped it in paper, wrote their name on the package, and took it to the butcher at the company store. He kept it in his cooler for them.

She explained the situation. She was certain the butter was okay. The problem was that she knew about the mouse. So would he just exchange her butter for someone else's? They would never know the difference, and she would feel much better.

"I understand," the butcher said. "Glad to help out." Disappearing into the back of the shop, he returned shortly and handed over a package. It was wrapped in the familiar paper with her handwriting on it. But she could see it was not the one she had brought in.

She went home happy, taking her tainted butter with her. Later the butcher told my grandmother what he'd done. He unwrapped great grandmother's package, rewrapped it, and gave it back to her.

4 *Glad We Went to Mariager*

The woman who seated us looked at our flushed, sweating faces, disappeared into the kitchen, and returned promptly with a large, chilled bowl of rabarbar grød and a pitcher of fresh cream.

I was surprised and delighted. I knew three words

of Danish. Two were rabarbar grød. My grand-mother had grown up in a Danish speaking home in Cambria, Wyoming. Rabarbar grød —a refresh-ing dish made from rhubarb juice and corn starch —was a family favorite.

This was in 1960. Since morning we had been wandering the byways of Mariager, a scenic village in northern Denmark dating back to the 15th cen-tury. The town had done an excellent job of turn-ing itself into an attractive tourist destination. The old part of town was protected by city ordinances that required property owners to preserve the medieval character of their buildings.

We had come to Mariager by happenchance. When we got off the train in Copenhagen the previous week, we went to the traveler information booth. We told the woman behind the counter we'd like to spend a few days in a small town off the beaten track. She sent us to Mariager.

After three pleasant days we left Mariager, made our way back to the beaten track by hitching a ride on a local freight barge, and checked into a hotel in Hobro. I mailed a postcard to my grandmother in Riverton, Wyoming.

Her response, a two sentence letter, was waiting a few weeks later at American Express in Zurich. "When you were in Hobro you should have gone to Mariager. That's where our family came from."

When we returned to Wyoming, my grandmother

started talking about the family's history. None of us had heard the stories before. Grandma had kept quiet all those years because she was embarrassed about coming from immigrant stock.

We knew we were Danish, that's all. But when I got back to Wyoming, Grandma started telling family stories.

5 *Tipoldermoder Buys a Ticket to America*

Three events relocated our family from Denmark to Wyoming.

First . . .

In the early 1890s my great-great-grandfather— or Tipoldefader—was one of the town drunks in Mariager, a small village in Denmark. To keep the children fed and shod his wife—our Tipoldemoder —hand laundered other people's soiled clothing and bedding. As women in that predicament have always done, she hid money from her husband.

One day an ocean liner tied up at the Mariager dock. The price of passage to America was posted. Tipoldefader was on a binge. Tipoldemoder packed a bag, dug into her hidden savings, strode down to the dock, and bought a ticket.

The next morning Tipoldefader woke up alone. And hung over. And seasick. He was emigrating to America. Everything he owned was in the bag Tipoldemoder had put aboard with him.

Then . . .

Tipoldefader landed in New York and turned up later in Texas. Nothing is known today of the intervening period.

According to family lore, in Texas he worked as a cowboy, was gored by a longhorn, and spent three months in bed with nothing to do but contemplate his life. He left the hospital reformed and sober. He hadn't intended to emigrate. Perhaps he hadn't intended to dry out either. But he stayed on the wagon the rest of his life.

Third . . .

In the meantime, significant economic events had been occurring in northeastern Wyoming. A few years earlier construction of the nascent Burlington Northern Railroad had stalled at Alliance, Nebraska, on its way to connecting with the Northern Pacific in Billings. The trains had outdistanced their coal sources.

Intensive prospecting turned up major deposits of high quality anthracite eight miles north of Newcastle. Within two years the Cambria Fuel Company had established a technologically innovative mining and coking operation there. To build a stable work force, it imported whole families from Europe.

Tipoldefader made his way north from Texas and went to work for the mines. After a time he arranged for Tipoldemoder and the kids to come over with one of the immigrant parties sponsored by the Company.

6 *An Empty Place at the Table*

When the family sat down to the feast at Thanksgiving in Riverton, Aunt Eleanor would always say, "This year I'm going to eat slow and a long time." My cousin Jim would always say, "Mom, you always say that."

Then one Thanksgiving, when Aunt Eleanor said "This year I'm going to eat slow and a long time," silence flooded the dining room. A place at the table had not been set for Jim, and never would be again.

Aunt Eleanor never again said, "This year I'm going to eat slow and a long time." And every Thanksgiving the rest of us heard her not say it and remembered why she didn't.

7 That Night on Cow Island

There's an island in Jackson Lake north of Colter Bay, directly off Leeks Marina, named Cow Island. Until that night in 1948, my mother had never heard of Cow Island.

We were staying at the old Leeks Lodge. As usual she and her friend returned late from Jackson, expecting to find me asleep. Instead she found a note on my pillow. "I'm on Cow Island. Donnie."

Certain questions came to mind. Where, and what, was Cow Island? Why had her 11 year old son gone to Cow Island? What was he doing there? Who was he with? How did he get there? How would he get back? When?

The next morning, in time for breakfast, one of the fishing guides from the lodge took a boat over to Cow Island and brought me back to the dock, sleeping bag in hand.

My mother had been leaving me alone at the resort every day while she and her companion went to Jackson. I'd hang around at the fishing guides' cabin at the dock. One of the guides suggested I camp overnight on Cow Island and offered to take me there. He said I'd have to leave a note for my mother though. He may have been trying to teach her a lesson about child neglect.

Long before the term "free range parenting" was invented, my mother was good at it. We lived in Casper at the time. She worked nights. I attended school during the day and set pins at the bowling alley afterward. She never got home before 2:00 a.m. Some nights I depended on that.

I would be asleep when she came home. She would be asleep when I left in the morning. Though we lived in the same house, we seldom saw each other from Monday through Saturday. She made a special effort to spend some time with me on Sundays.

When my mother was at work in Casper, she could only assume I was at home. But that night 70 years ago at Leeks Lodge, she knew for certain where I was. I was on Cow Island.

8 *Mom Said She Often Married*

My mother's life ended in her early forties. Half a century later questions remain. All those claimed marriages, for instance. Did they actually take place? With a license and everything? One wonders too about the requisite divorces.

I can confirm from memory two of the first three purported weddings.

I know Mom married her third husband, Ray Upton, because I was present at the ceremony. Ray chartered a small twin engine plane to fly us and a pair of their friends to Las Vegas from Phoenix. He and Mom were married there by a justice of the peace.

Six months later my mother and I were on a Greyhound headed back to Wyoming. While living in Phoenix I had turned ten years old. Had learned how to swim, having spent the summer alone at the public pool. Had experienced ethnicity, having lived in an impoverished area of the city. Had a startling but harmless encounter with a pederast. And was returning to Wyoming familiar with the concept of domestic violence.

Ray had once been fired from his job for excessive brutality. That was not an easy standard to meet in the Los Angeles Police Department.

Before Ray, Mom married Keith Ricks, nicknamed "Gandhi" because he was so skinny. The ceremony was conducted in Jackson by Gandhi's cousin, who was bishop of the LDS stake I was told later.

I was three, maybe four at the time. From the day of the wedding I remember this: several children and I were chasing each other on a lawn, driving ourselves wild with excitement. We were all dressed in better clothes than usual and, as we played, we knew we would soon be called inside by the adults. Something important was about to happen.

So I can attest to Mom's second marriage (to Gandhi) as well as her third (to Ray). But was there a first marriage? Mom and Max Crowe, my father, probably did get married, though that's not certain. There are two documents that seem to attest to the marriage, although neither can be considered conclusive.

Max's name appears on my birth certificate. Wyoming law at the time required doctors to ask for proof of marriage before naming the father on a birth certificate. But that evidence is uncertain. Small town family physicians would have understood it was best sometimes to dispense with formalities.

Also, a wedding announcement appeared in the newspaper. The clipping turned up decades later, after my maternal grandmother died, among some old family photos and documents.

Grandma had written the announcement. She said that Max and Rhoda, to the total surprise of family and friends, had run off to Idaho and gotten married, secretly. The wedding was said to have occurred on a certain date a certain number of months previously—carefully checked for accuracy we can assume. Or at least for sufficiency.

Some people in Riverton may not yet have heard

that Rhoda Parker had been knocked up by one of the Crowe boys. But everyone knew after Grandma announced the event in the paper.

9 *The Train Didn't Stop at Shoshoni Any More*

In 1889 rancher Bryant B. Brooks guided a party of hunters on a six week round trip by horseback between Casper and Dubois. Afterward he wrote, "Do you know about the 150 mile stretch between Casper and Lander? If not you have missed nothing."

Seven decades later nothing much had changed, except people could drive or take the train.

We can assume the soldier, being young, untraveled, and from the Deep South, had never before stared out a train window for hours without seeing anything green. He likely never stared out without seeing ... anything. That was likely how it seemed to him anyway.

The dry Wyoming hills ran off to the horizon, where they sometimes disappeared into the shadows of distant mountain ranges. Outcrops of weathered sandstone relieved the eye now and then. Hundreds of square miles of sage brush grew under an immense dome of pale blue, yielding infrequent glimpses of human effect.

The young soldier's khaki uniform, distinguished only by a single stripe on the sleeve and a parachute qualification badge, was rumpled. Like him, it had an odor after three days and two nights riding in coaches. But the trip would end soon. The orders he carried, signed by his commanding officer, declared he would be met at the railroad station at Shoshoni, Wyoming.

Neither he nor his CO were aware that the railroad, when it ended passenger service to Riverton and Lander years before, abandoned Shoshoni as well. Shoshoni Siding, several miles from town, existed primarily as the location where the main track, west bound from Casper, turned north through Wind River Canyon into the Big Horn Basin. Shoshoni Siding was nothing but a single building, a small brown passenger station boarded up and padlocked, in a vast emptiness. Trains stopped there; but only by special arrangement.

When thinking back on that day, I've wondered what apprehensions the tired young soldier felt as the air brakes hissed and the line of cars shuddered to a halt. He saw two vehicles waiting next to the empty station. Three people stood beside the sedan, a middle aged couple who were likely the parents and a young man his age. Two gentlemen wearing dark suits and ties stood next to the hearse.

The young soldier said later he hadn't known my

cousin, Jim Ridgeway, that well. Jim was just a big cheerful kid in the same mortar platoon at Ft. Bragg, with a crooked grin and dedicated to partying. Others hesitated when the First Sgt. asked for a volunteer to serve as escort. The young soldier quickly raised his hand. A paid trip to the Wild West would be a welcome break from training.

In those days young men drafted into the Army did not die fighting wars in distant lands. But they sometimes died in dumb accidents on military bases at home.

Backcountry Patrol, Grand Tetons, 1959

1 The Snow Shovel at the Top of the Pole   2 Lucky I Could Saddle a Horse

3 The Cowboy Didn't Like Me. He had a Gun

4 Messed Up My First Chance to Write a Citation   5 My Packhorses Bolt

6 Had on My Smokey Bear Hat, at Least   7 The Earth Moved for All Three of Us

8 Two Crimes Against Nature   9 Clearing Up Some False GTNP History

10 Three Horses Going Two Ways on a One-way Trail   11 Spud Sees a Bear

12 The Hero Who Taught Me How to Pack   13 The Wolverine

14 A Moose Changes My Mind   15 The False Alarm Fire

16 The Horse Trains the Rider   17 Camp Near Water, the Fire Guard Said

18 Remember the Slop Bucket?   19 Reporting My Patrol Results

20 Ever Hear about the Other Yellowstone Earthquake?

21 Sure, the Rangers Had a Gun Back Then

PHOTO. Spud, my replacement saddle horse, at the Death Canyon Ranger Station in 1959. A shy little bay who was bullied by other horses, he seemed content spending the summer alone in the mountains with me.

1 The Snow Shovel at the Top of the Pole

Sitting on the doorstep of the patrol cabin in Grand Teton's upper Granite Canyon after supper, I watched a young bull moose skulking thirty yards away. Unaware of me, he was sneaking up on Spud and Sandy, unaware of him, as they grazed on their picket ropes in a small meadow near the creek. Curiosity satisfied, he wandered off.

That was the summer of 1959. The Park Service had purchased the Granite Canyon drainage from the State of Wyoming only recently, acquiring the patrol cabin too. The sturdy little cabin, eight feet by twelve, had been built as a winter shelter for state game wardens. They had used it when patrolling the backcountry to prevent illegal trapping of fur bearing animals. As the first park service ranger assigned to patrol the south end of Grand Teton, I had been sent to locate the cabin and assess its condition.

An evocative sight was waiting as I rode up to the cabin that afternoon. A 20-foot lodgepole pine was nailed vertically next to the door. A snow shovel was wired to the top.

We can imagine a robust man, after a hard day patrolling on skis or snowshoes, arriving in the general area of the cabin. He would be facing early darkness and a disheartening prospect. Unless he found shelter, he would spend a long, cold night out of doors.

His first task would be to locate the cabin, which would be buried deep under the snow. Then he would need to find the door. That shovel protruding into the air, and the pole leading down into the snow, would have solved both problems. A snug roof, four thick walls, a hot stove, a kerosene lamp, and a bear trap cot would be his for the digging.

I didn't realize, as I sat on the stoop that quiet summer evening watching the curious young moose, I had become a small footnote in the history of Grand Teton National Park. I was wrapping up day two of the first ever park service patrol of what would be called, years later, the Teton Crest Trail.

2 *Lucky I Could Saddle a Horse*

I had been a university graduate almost a whole month. (UW, English Lit.)

When I reported for duty as a seasonal ranger in Grand Teton, park management recognized my special qualification . . . I knew how to saddle a horse. So they stationed me in a cabin up in Death Canyon and assigned me to backcountry patrol. They said they'd pay me even.

That was the best job, and best summer, of my life.

Today in Grand Teton, hikers are advised to arrive early at the Death Canyon trailhead. The parking lot at White Grass Ranger Station fills up quickly.

Parking was not a problem six decades ago, when I was the first ranger stationed in the Death Canyon Ranger Station. The trail crew maintained the trails. Otherwise headquarters knew little about what was going on in the south end of the park.

Upper Death Canyon, and Alaska Basin north of it, were seldom visited. To the south the Granite Canyon watershed, purchased from the State of Wyoming, had only recently been incorporated into the park. My initial patrol was the park's first official demonstration of stewardship there.

My primary duty as a horse patrol ranger was to look after people and premises. But I was also told to report on visitor activities and count heads. When I turned in my log at the end of the season, the total came to fewer than 50 people.

3 *The Cowboy Didn't Like Me. He had a Gun*

I was wearing a uniform shirt, a smoky bear hat, and the badge of a National Park Service Ranger. As I rode toward Grand Teton's new south boundary on the upper Granite Canyon trail, two riders entered the park from the other direction.

The first was dressed like an old time cowboy, complete with a six shooter strapped to his hip. He (like me) was leading a pack horse.

The man following behind, bland in a tan windbreaker and khakis, was bare headed and pudgy. He wore hiking boots that didn't fit his stirrups. He rode with reins in one hand and saddle horn in the other.

The sight of me angered the cowboy. At the time the population of Jackson Hole seemed divided into three groups: some loved the Park; some hated it; and a whole lot of people thought the Park, on balance, was a reasonably good idea. They'd rather talk about something else for change.

Some old timers—the cowboy I met that day, for

instance—got riled when they came face to face on the trail with a young park ranger. There I was, government overreach made manifest.

The dude, on the other hand, looked puzzled. He was paying big money to be packed into the mountains as a lone guest. He had been promised wilderness. Straightaway he encounters law and order.

4 *Messed Up My First Chance to Write a Citation*

I had ridden up to the cabin in Death Canyon, inventoried its contents, and was heading back with a list of gear and supplies to pack in for the rest of the summer.

I came across a dozen dismounted riders at the spot where the creek, after meandering through the upper canyon, drops steeply into the lower canyon. The people were milling around, loud and boisterous. They had braved the cliff hugging trail up from Phelps Lake.

Guests at a dude ranch, they were guided by a pair of young wranglers. They were also escorted—in clear violation of park regulations—by a happy black and white cattle dog, tongue hanging, running excited circles among all those legs.

I sat my horse as the wranglers, standing by my left stirrup, looked up. They were smiling but apprehensive. They tried to seem nonchalant about the dog, shooing him away unobtrusively. They cast furtive glances at me, wondering whether I had noticed the dog; or whether, being a seasonal, I was even aware of the prohibition against unleashed pets in the Park.

After a few minutes of friendly, get-acquainted chatting, I reined my horse around to head down the canyon. Out of the corner of my eye, I saw the wranglers exchange relieved grins.
Then I stopped, turned in the saddle, and said, "Next time, leave the dog at home."

Word apparently got out. A ranger was now stationed in Death Canyon. He was a seasonal but okay. At the end of August I turned in a blank citation book. Never got another chance to write one.

5 *My Packhorses Bolt*

I reined King toward the trail to the Death Canyon Ranger Station, five miles away in the mountains. The two packhorses turned to follow. I was moving in for the summer.

Under their pack tarps the pack horses carried

oats, a bedroll, clothing, and odds and ends of equipment and supplies. Sandy's right side box was filled with groceries. His left box was empty, but a folding steel cot was lashed to the outside.

The horses were well sweated from the steep climb up the canyon when we got to the ranger station. I tied King to a tree and Sandy to the hitching rail spiked to the cabin wall.

Then I made a greenhorn mistake. I tied the mare to the other end of the same rail.

When I unlashed the cot and lifted it off the pannier, Sandy rolled back an eye, let out a what-the-hell-is-that? snort, and reared. The mare, panicked by his panic, reared too. Together they jerked the hitching rail off the cabin and, dragging it between them, stampeded into the pines by the corral.

The rail broke as the horses passed on each side of a tree, freeing them from each other. The pannier on Sandy's right side shattered against another tree, sending groceries flying. Both horses disappeared upstream into the timber.

Glimpses of a meadow were visible beyond the trees. Walking up the trail toward it, I was unsure what to do. I was especially concerned that the horses might circle around me and head back down the canyon together. Having my packhorses show up back at White Grass unattended, the mare still carrying full paniers, would not make a good impression first day on the job.

The mare stood trembling just inside the meadow, still tied to her half the rail. As I took her halter rope and calmed her, I could see Sandy further on, head up and looking back, trotting in circles.

Tying the mare to a tree near the cabin, I went back for Sandy. He had slowed to a walk and was puffing heavily. Taking his head, I discovered why he had kept running. The smashed pannier had snagged on the pack rope and, dragging behind, had been chasing him around and around the meadow.

When the horses were unpacked, unsaddled, watered, and snuffling in their oat boxes in the corral, I gathered groceries scattered among the trees. Odds and ends kept turning up all summer, including a can of corned beef I came across at the end of August, the day before I left the ranger station for the last time.

6   *Had on My Smokey Bear Hat, at Least*

The summer of 1959 I lived alone in the mountains, a young backcountry patrol ranger in Grand Teton. One afternoon intruders entered my ranger station.

That morning I had saddled Spud and patrolled up

the north side of Death Canyon to the Static Peak Divide. Rain fell steadily as we came back down late in the afternoon. We were home and Spud, watered at the creek and wiped down, was munching at his oat box in the corral.

Leaving a track of muddy boot prints from the door to the cook stove, I had started a fire and the cabin was beginning to warm. I dug out some dry clothes and began to strip off my wet ones. I was standing in the stork position, my jeans off one leg but still around the ankle of the other, when the door opened and two young women walked in. They were backpackers who had come down the trail behind us.

The moment was disconcerting. Few people showed up in the south end of the park in those days, and none had ever come into the ranger station without knocking. Our ranger orientation had not covered what to do if young women entered our post while we were not wearing pants.

But at least I was still wearing my soaked ranger shirt. And my badge. And my smoky bear hat.

The women said they were going to set up camp a short distance down the trail.

The next story reports what happened that night.

7 *The Earth Moved for All Three of Us*

I had neighbors the night the big Yellowstone earthquake struck. They were two young women who surprised me that afternoon by walking into the ranger station while I was changing into dry clothes after a rainy patrol. They told me they were going to camp a couple of hundred yards further along the trail at the overlook above Phelps Lake.

That night strange events began to occur in the dark. Out in the corral Spud whinnied anxiously. Engrossed in a book, I was slow to grasp what was happening.

The logs of the wall across the room shifted back and forth. Myriad small lights scurried around the cabin as the Coleman lantern swung from its hook above my head. The chair jolted under me. Behind the cabin, loose boulders rattled down the 1,500 foot cliff on Prospector Mountain.

The quake lasted 30 - 40 seconds. I took sugar cubes out to comfort Spud, then walked down the trail to check on the neighbors. They were elated, ecstatic.

That was the final camp of their trip. They had spent the evening rehearsing the stories they would tell when they got back to New Jersey, tales of their adventures while backpacking among the high peaks. (Including, probably, an account of walking unannounced into a back country ranger station.)

Now they could also tell their friends about surviving a strong earthquake . . . on the ground in their sleeping bags . . . in a place called Death Canyon.

8 *Two Crimes Against Nature*

When I was a young seasonal ranger in Grand Teton in the 1950s, a permanent park employee and his family committed a crime against nature, then tried to redeem themselves by committing a worse one.

That family, like many before and since, had to leave their dog behind when the park service transferred them from Washington DC to Jackson Hole. Employees residing in national parks were forbidden to have domestic pets, period.

Then one day they announced they had acquired a pet after all. But it was "legal" they insisted, because it belonged to a species indigenous to the park. They had been given a newborn coyote pup.

The pup may have been a wild animal genetically; but behaviorally it became a domesticated house pet the instant they stuck a nipple in its mouth. The coyote pup socialized quickly, may have imprinted on humans. He liked being petted. He connected readily, even with strangers. The whole neighborhood soon came to love him.

Every afternoon the school bus pulled up at the entrance to the residential area. The pup's favorite event of the day was to meet the kids and play-fully escort them to their homes. He put on weight quickly, however. He soon started knocking children down. He never really bit a child, but he nipped and grabbed and dragged.

No viciousness was involved. The pup pranced around and tussled with the kids in pure fun. He was wired to romp aggressively with a den of litter mates who were exercising the musculature and nervous systems that, as predators, they would need when they started learning to kill for a living.

The family announced they had decided "to return the coyote to the wild" at a remote spot in the national forest. That of course was a death sentence. The only uncertainties were how the coyote would die and how much he would suffer first.

He would likely starve, having never been taught to hunt. Or he might be killed by other coyotes, who would never tolerate a stranger in their midst who had not mastered the deference behaviors required by pack structure. Or, being so thoroughly socialized, he might happily run up to greet a human carrying a gun.

The family, having betrayed the coyote by domesticating him, should have accepted responsibility for their error. They should have borne the anguish and had the pup euthanized.

On the other hand . . . maybe they did have him euthanized. Perhaps claiming they were releasing him was just a cover story to ease the mixed emotions the pup had stirred in their family and the community as a whole.

❖ ❖ ❖

9 *Clearing Up Some False GTNP History*

Remember the good old days, when people took pride in being truthful? When facts were honored? When we laughed at those who spoke b.s. and distained those who told partisan lies?

Here's the truth, and the facts, regarding a contentious issue in the history of Jackson Hole and Grand Teton National Park.

The truth: When Grand Teton was consolidating in the 1950s and 60s, the Park Service did not force old time ranch families off their land, nor did it pressure them to sell.

The facts: The Park Service respected the feelings of those who were reluctant to sell their family's heritage and children's birthright. It offered them a deal some people found hard to refuse. That is . . .

The Park offered to buy their land outright after an equitable price had been negotiated, one reasonably consistent with the appraised value.

The Park then would lease the land back to the family for $1.00 a year.

The term of the lease was until the passing of the second generation. That is, the sellers could bank the money immediately, then continue to operate the ranch and live out their lives on the property. Then their offspring would inherit the lease and could do the same. When the last of the second generation died, the lease would expire. Some of those leases may still be in force today.

The only way the Park Service could have exerted pressure on landowners would be to threaten to declare eminent domain. There was no way the federal government was going to get sucked into that political quagmire.

Here's my source . . .

Conversations 60 years ago with Maynard B. Barrows (1906-1975). From the mid '50s through the mid '60s, Barrows was the Park Service's assigned negotiator for the acquisition of parcels of land within the GTNP boundary that were still held in private hands. "Infills" they were called.

He was the NW Region Forester at the time, stationed at Moose. He had been a young ranger in Yellowstone after the Interior Dept. took over the park from the Army and was Chief Ranger there in the 40s. Born, raised, and educated in Colorado, he was a native westerner who understood westerners, their values, and their culture.

He also happened to be my father in law.

❖ ❖ ❖

10   *Three Horses Going Two Ways on a One-way Trail*

One fine day in June, 1959, I moved into a backcountry ranger station in Grand Teton, the one up in Death Canyon. The next morning I headed King back down the trail, the two pack horses following with empty panniers. My mind wandered. I should have been paying attention.

Suddenly everything was wrong. Both packhorses were beside me instead of strung out behind. They were still headed downhill. But I was looking uphill. We were stopped side by side facing in different directions, three horses wide on a one-horse trail, high up on the precipitous canyon wall.

Then I understood. I had been warned that King's right foreleg was suspect. I was told to try him out and, if I reported him unsound, he would be exchanged for a different saddle horse.

Now we were in a tangle on the trail because King, his leg tender from the previous day's work, had decided he'd rather go uphill. Noticing me woolgathering, he took the opportunity to turn back. And he picked a narrow spot on the trail to do it.

The horses, even the knot head Sandy, recognized the situation was dire. King froze. The packhorses, rolling their eyes at the abyss falling away half a step to their right, skittered to the left against King, then froze too.

I was trapped in the saddle. Sandy's pannier jammed my left knee against King, and King jammed my right knee against the granite cliff. Speaking reassuringly to the horses while wiggling free of my stirrups, I squeezed down between King and Sandy. Carefully separating the three, I got the pack string realigned and headed downhill again.

King was a willing worker with a fine temperament. A big black half Morgan with a star and stockings, he and a smoky bear hat made handsome accessories for a young ranger, I thought. But King never again challenged the steep trail into Death Canyon.

11 *Spud Sees a Bear*

I came to work Monday after our three horse tangle on the Death Canyon trail the preceding Friday. King and the pack mare were gone from the White Grass Ranger Station. A new saddle horse, Spud, was in the corral with Sandy. For the rest of the summer he and I patrolled the Grand Teton backcountry together.

Spud was a nondescript little bay, 14 hands, who was sound, a hard worker, and devoted. Bullied at the ranch by the other horses, he seemed content living alone in the mountains with me.

The morning I took delivery of Spud, we headed out for his first climb into Death Canyon. He stopped abruptly a quarter mile from White Grass. He waited calmly while a cinnamon bear ambled out of the brush and crossed the trail 15 yards ahead of us. I let Spud decide when he felt safe to proceed. He moved on almost immediately. I was impressed.

He could be startled though. He reared one day when a pair of hikers, napping under a spruce next to the trail, surprised us both by sitting up suddenly. The saddle horn caught me squarely in the sternum, cracking it. For a couple of weeks, getting up from the cot in the morning was the hardest work I did all day.

Spud and I learned to trust each other. When time came for lunch on patrols, I'd find him a patch of grass, loosen his cinch, hang his bridle on the saddle horn, and leave him to graze. I'd look for a shady spot near the creek where I would eat and, sometimes, take a twenty-minute snooze. When I woke Spud would be waiting a few steps away.

12 *The Hero Who Taught Me How to Pack*

In the rear view mirror I saw a green park service pickup turn behind me onto the dirt road to the White Grass Ranger Station. It was pulling a horse trailer.

That would be Stan Spurgeon, the Assistant Chief Ranger, Grand Teton NP, who was bringing a second pack horse for me. That day I was moving into the backcountry ranger station in Death Canyon.

Stan started with the Park Service as a teenage horse packer and worked his way up through the ranger ranks. A victim of seniority by the time I knew him, he was doing most of his rangering from a desk.

His eyes lit a few days earlier when he promised to come to the Death Canyon trailhead to help me pack the horses. We both understood that "help" meant "teach."

Some people may recall that two rangers drowned in the Snake River late in the winter of 1960, and that a third ranger tried desperately to save them. That survivor was Stan. In the linked account of the event below, Stan is referred to, anonymously, as the Assistant Chief Ranger.

Stan probably insisted the story be written that way. He would have considered his efforts that day a failure, not a heroic effort.

http://www.odmp.org/officer/14167-district-ran-ger-gale-h-wilcox#ixzz3yHXVzaax

13 *The Wolverine*

Two versions of the story circulated in Grand Teton park headquarters. Those who knew me said, "Don saw a wolverine at Marion Lake." Others said, "That seasonal up in Death Canyon claims he saw a wolverine at Marion Lake." They assumed I had seen only a marmot.

The uncertainty was understandable. The year was 1959. The last reported wolverine sighting in the Lower 48—except for Glacier National Park along the Canadian border—dated from more than 25 years earlier, before the war.

Marion Lake is nestled above timberline in a bowl between the headwaters of Death and Granite canyons. A tall cliff rises on the west side. I had just finished setting up camp on the east side of the lake among the spruce near the shore. Spud and Sandy were grazing in a meadow nearby on their picket ropes.

Across the lake stones rattled in the scree at the base of the cliff. Then a second time. My binoculars picked out a movement. It was a wolverine turning over rocks, hunting rodents. I watched for probably half an hour. The clatter resumed as the sun came up the next morning. Again, I was treated to an extended viewing.

My report was a big event at park headquarters. The sighting was officially recorded even though not everyone concurred. Since I was alone at the time, the sighting was designated unconfirmed.

It was upgraded to confirmed that September, after the season ended. Four hikers from the Sierra Club hurried into the visitors' center and excitedly reported they had seen a wolverine while camped at Marion Lake.

Needless to say, the wolverine I saw wasn't the first one to return to the Grand Teton area. Several people who lived in Jackson Hole during those years have since told me they saw wolverines around that time too. My report was just the first one to be officially recognized.

The experts who worked for the Park Service were reluctant to credit wildlife sightings from unqualified people, those who had only grown up in the mountains.

When I reported the wolverine sighting, my boss Doug Maclaren, who was the district ranger, quizzed me closely. He finally seemed convinced. But then he said, "Wait . . . have you ever actually seen a wolverine before?"

My answer: "For four years I played football for the Riverton Wolverines. We had a stuffed one in our trophy case."

14   *A Moose Changes My Mind*

The coffee pot was starting to boil on the wood stove behind me. I stood at the open door of the upper Granite Canyon patrol cabin contemplating the steep slope across the creek. I wondered. If I go over the mountain, what will I see?

Earlier I had watered the horses and moved their picket stakes to fresh grass. After breakfast I found a place to cross the creek and started to hike up toward the ridge on the south side of the canyon.

Quartering back and forth as I climbed the steep slope, I spotted a cow moose meandering and browsing further uphill, a calf at her side. I kept changing direction trying to avoid her, but our routes continued to cross.

The distance between us narrowed. The moose became agitated. The other side of the mountain lost its allure. I turned back.

I know now what was on the other side of that mountain. Jackson Hole. Jackson Hole as viewed from the ridge above what was to become, 40 years later, the Teton Village ski development.

15 *The False Alarm Fire*

That Tuesday morning in Grand Teton in 1959 I was hungover. But I wasn't AWOL. Not strictly speaking. I just wasn't where everyone thought I was, including my boss the district ranger.

He believed I was deep in the mountains at the backcountry ranger station where I'd been posted, about to begin my 8:00 to 5:00 workday. But I was somewhere else, having deviated from my usual schedule—afterhours and for reasons that were entirely my own business.

On Mondays my usual work log showed me riding the trail between the White Grass and Death Canyon ranger stations three times. I'd arrive at White Grass with my week's supply of groceries in the trunk of the car, plus fresh laundry and a bag of oats. I'd pack it all to the ranger station five miles up in Death Canyon, return the pack horse to the corral at White Grass, and finish the day by riding up the canyon again. As my boss instructed, those 15 miles on horseback were entered into my daily log as three patrols.

That was my usual routine. But I'd been invited to a birthday party that Monday night. The celebration would take place near Jenny Lake at the ranch used by the family from Idaho who trucked horses into the park every summer and took tourists on trail rides. They also leased a few horses to the park.

The party was expected to run late and liquor would be served. I'd been invited to sleep over in the bunk house.

So that Monday I packed in my groceries as usual, worked several hours on a carpentry project at the ranger station, then finished the day by patrolling the trail down to White Grass, the packhorse following with empty panniers. First thing next day I planned to patrol back to my ranger station.

Tuesday morning I sat down with the ranch hands to a strong cup of coffee and a plate of bacon, eggs, and hot cakes. One of the brothers in the family barged in. "Hey, did you guys hear what happened in Death Canyon? The ranger station burned down, and they can't find the ranger."

He almost had me. My gut clenched as a shot of adrenaline surged through my system. But I'd been jobbed before. The dining room was quiet as everyone watched, waiting for my reaction. I pondered his announcement for several seconds. Then I asked: "Can I borrow a saddle horse? I'd better ride up by way of Cascade Canyon and crawl in under the ashes."

◆ ◆ ◆

16 *The Horse Trains the Rider*

When I was stationed in Grand Teton's Death Canyon as a young back country patrol ranger, park headquarters outfitted us with rent-a-horse mounts leased from a concessionaire at Jenny Lake.

Sandy was the horse I packed with. Unlike King, my first saddle horse, and Spud, the replacement I was assigned when King proved unsound, Sandy did not have a good attitude. He was accustomed to carrying inexperienced tourists on trail rides. He preferred easy days of strolling from here to there and back, nose to tail with horses he knew, while mostly ignoring whoever happened to be in the saddle and holding the reins.

Sandy was corralled at White Grass Ranger Station, where I left my car while in the mountains. When I didn't need him for packing, the Fire Guard stationed there used him as a saddle horse. They patrolled the flat trails along the base of the Grand Teton range.

The young Fire Guard was . . . well . . . citified, you might say.

He told me that Sandy had started out as a willful and frustrating mount. But they worked out an understanding. When they set out in the morning, he would point Sandy down the intended trail—then slack the reins. Sandy would amble and graze, taking life easy, until time came to turn back. (That decision, I gathered, was usually made by the rider, though sometimes by the horse.) Then Sandy would hurry home to his oats and corral.

The Fire Guard was proud of himself for negotiating a sensible compromise with his mount. I was impressed by Sandy's teaching skills.

17 *Camp Near Water, the Fire Guard Said*

A party of six rode up to the ranger station in Death Canyon, with three pack horses following. The man in the lead dismounted, angry and looking for a confrontation. Anyone wearing a Park uniform would do. I stepped out the door.

"Why does the Park Service hire idiots like that Fire Guard down at White Grass? Is it official policy? Do they go out of their way to find people like him?"

"What's he done this time?"

"Just look . . . Me. My wrangler. Four guests. Six saddle horses and three pack horses. And that silly son-of-a-bitch told me I should camp near water."

I laughed. Holding out my hand to shake his, I said, "Well now, I'm sure you're all going to be sleeping next to the creek tonight. No point in letting good advice go to waste."

He glared at me. Then he started laughing too. The rest of his day went better I think.

In fairness to the Fire Guard, he was parroting his superiors at headquarters. They had instructed him to warn people headed into the back country to camp near water. Back packers carried their water, and some liked to spend nights high up on the dry ridges. Abandoned campfires had been found smoldering because the canteens were empty the next morning.

But the Fire Guard should have had better sense than to tell someone leading a party on horseback and a pack string to camp near water.

◆ ◆ ◆

18 *Remember the Slop Bucket?*

When we hear of people who live without plumbing, toilets that were not designed to flush, or worse, come to mind. We also think of fresh water being hand carried into the house from another location. But does anyone today wonder how, after use, the grey water used to get back out of the house? Those of us who have been there, done that, know. We remember the slop bucket.

The slop bucket was often a five gallon motor oil container, repurposed. Like today's sink drain, the slop bucket was where the dregs from coffee cups went, and shaving water. After we rinsed vegetables or brushed our teeth we added to the contents of the slop bucket. And that's where we poured the dirty dish water. When the bucket was full it was carried outside to be emptied.

One night in 1959, in the backcountry ranger station in Grand Teton's Death Canyon, I was negligent. As I got ready for bed I noticed the slop bucket was almost full. I decided to leave it until morning.

The next morning my only companion in the mountains that summer—other than Spud, my saddle horse—was floating in the slop bucket, drowned. He or she was a pretty little deer mouse who showed up regularly after supper, nibbled at whatever small treat I had left out, then spent a busy evening scurrying around the cabin while I read under the Coleman lantern.

Probably that night a morsel of food had been floating in the slop bucket, just far enough down from the edge to be tempting, but too far to climb back out.

19   *Reporting My Patrol Results*

The summer of 1959 I was a seasonal ranger assigned to backcountry horse patrol in Grand Teton National Park. I was posted to the relatively remote Death Canyon Ranger Station, where my patrol area included what today is called the Teton Crest Trail.

Doug McLaren, the district ranger and my boss, gave me instructions for a three day patrol that would be the Park Service's first official presence in the newest addition to the park. The drainage of Granite Canyon Creek, the southernmost portion of the park, had only recently been acquired from the State of Wyoming. No one working at park headquarters at the time had yet been to Granite Canyon.

Doug gave me a list of jobs to do. The following week I reported to his office and we checked off my patrol results.

At Marion Lake I had seen a wolverine. Four hikers who camped at Marion Lake a few weeks later reporting seeing it too. That turned out to be the first confirmed sighting of a wolverine south of Glacier National Park since before the War. Doug hadn't put that on my list, but I reported it anyway.

I had located the upper Granite Canyon patrol cabin, spent a night there, and assessed its condition as excellent and usable.

I had found a developed, though rough, camp site near the headwaters of Granite Canyon Creek. It had been heavily used by horse packers, apparently for years. Likely it was a spot where dude ranches packed in guests. It had probably been a hunting camp too, when the State had jurisdiction.

When Doug asked how many people I had counted, I told him about meeting a wrangler who was guiding a lone dude. "And how many more people did you see?"

"None."

"You saw only two people up there? In three days?"

"That's right."

Then he asked how much trash I'd hauled out on my pack horse.

I was pleased again to report, "None." The whole area was clean, even the scattered camp sites that had been used by hikers.

He stopped me as I started out the door.

"But did you look under the rocks?"

"Look under the rocks?"

"Back packers flatten their cans and hide them under rocks."

20 *Ever Hear about the Other Yellowstone Earthquake?*

That morning over breakfast in Riverton, I gave son Jim, 11 years old, a choice. We could stop in Grand Teton and hike up to the Death Canyon Ranger Station, where years before his dad spent a summer as a backcountry patrol ranger. Or we could drive on to Yellowstone and see the geysers. Geysers didn't stand a chance.

Now, after a satisfying day in Death Canyon bingeing on nostalgia, we were on the road again, weaving among the tourist vehicles. We were using Yellowstone as a through route into Montana.

As we drove, I told Jim about the Great Yellowstone Earthquake of 1959.

When out of the mountains we started getting radio reception again. The lead story in the local news that day—August 30, 1974—was that Yellowstone had been shaken by its first major earthquake since the big one in 1959. Jim and I felt nothing because we were on the highway when it happened.

21   *Sure, the Rangers Had a Gun Back Then*

Thirty five years had passed since I locked the Death Canyon Ranger Station for the last time and rode down the canyon, pack horse following behind.

Having dawdled over dinner at the Old Faithful Inn, Barbara and I were headed south on a dark moonless night. We were on our motorcycle, camping gear on the back. We intended to drive into Grand Teton then head east toward Togwotee Pass. I remembered a side road into the national forest where we could look for a place to pitch our tent.

The ranger in the booth at Yellowstone's south entrance signaled us to stop. He warned us to be on the lookout for a hitchhiker. A prisoner had escaped in Montana and law enforcement in the region was on general alert.

As we approached Moran Junction, red and blue flashing lights demanded another stop. I almost lost control of the bike when a powerful spotlight blinded me. The Grand Teton ranger aiming it said he was making sure I couldn't "see this."

"This" was a shotgun. I'd never seen an armed national park ranger before.

When I was a seasonal the summer of 1959, the only official firearm in Grand Teton was a .38 Police Special reportedly locked away in the safe in the Chief Ranger's office. We were told it was taken out once a year to be cleaned. Made sense that people who wore badges and enforced laws would have a gun somewhere on the premises.

After the ranger at Moran Junction sent us on our way, we exited the Park, turned south at the Hatchet Motel, and drove up the gravel road leading into the hills behind it. Google Earth shows that area logged off now.

After a mile or two the bike's head light picked out tire tracks leaving the road. We followed them to a small spring and a good place to camp.

In the morning we found ourselves high up in a large open meadow with a broad view of Jackson Hole to the west. The sun was rising over the Wind Rivers behind us. Barbara had never seen the Grand Tetons before.

A Kid In Dubois

PHOTO. Roundup time on the EA Ranch, 1950. I was the chore boy, only 13 but already six feet tall. That horse taught me my first lessons in how to work cattle.

1   Butch Cassidy, John D. Rockefeller Jr, my grandfather, me

A narrative thread, slender but certain, weaves Butch Cassidy, John D. Rockefeller Jr, my grandfather, and me into the history of western Wyoming.

In 1889, a few weeks after the bank in Telluride was robbed, Cassidy walked into the Amoretti bank in Lander and sat down with the young assistant manager, E. A. Amoretti Jr. When Cassidy left he had opened an account with a large cash deposit, had made a new friend, and had been hired to work on Amoretti's EA Ranch, five miles north of Dubois.

In 1922, the bad wagon road through Togwotee Pass was upgraded to a bad road for motor traffic. Amoretti established the Lander-Yellowstone Park Transportation Company. It hauled tourists from the Chicago & Northwestern terminal in Lander to Jackson Hole. He built the Brooks Lake Lodge for his guests, as well as the Amoretti Inn at Moran, near the site of what one day would become the Jackson Lake Lodge. My grandfather, Cody Simonson, was one of the young men in Dubois Amoretti hired to drive his motor stages.

In 1926, John D. Rockefeller Jr visited Jackson Hole with his family, noticed the Grand Tetons, and was inspired to create a national park. The historical record confirms they stayed at the Amoretti Inn. It does not disclose the name of their driver.

I wish I could report that, like Butch Cassidy and my grandfather, I once worked for Eugene Amoretti Jr also. But that would not be true. In 1950, when I was 13, Francis Amoretti hired me as chore boy for the summer on the EA Ranch. That was in June. Her husband had died in March.

2 Chore Boy, on the Payroll at the EA Ranch

In 1950, when I hired on as chore boy for the summer at the EA Ranch north of Dubois, the elegant Mrs. Francis Amoretti, 75, was my boss. Her daughter, Mrs. Eloise Peck, was my boss. Eloise's husband George was my boss. On a ranch everybody told the chore boy what to do, including the cook—especially the cook.

When life stirred in the four guest cabins in the morning, people could flush their toilets because the chore boy had been up before them to pull the starter rope on the one-cylinder gas engine that pressured the water system. They could take hot showers because earlier he had quietly stoked a coal fire in the water heater in the shed behind their cabins. He would do the same in the evening so they could go to bed clean.

When everyone sat down to breakfast—ranch management and guests in the dining room, hired hands and chore boy in the kitchen—their bacon, eggs, and flap jacks were cooked on a wood burning stove. The chore boy split the wood and kept the box filled.

Food was kept wholesome in a large ice box. Big blocks of ice, cut and hauled down from a high lake the previous winter, were buried under insulating sawdust in the ice house. Every third day the chore boy would dig out a block, split off a 50 pound piece, wash it, and take it to the house.

The chore boy's bosses seemed always to know of items that needed to be picked up, carried, and put down someplace else.

At roundup everyone pitched in. I learned to ride a cow pony hard and headlong through the sage brush, tight grip on the saddle horn. When a calf was roped and thrown my job was to secure the hind quarters while it was inoculated and branded, forcing the legs apart to present the bull calves for castration.

3 Why the Boedeckers Had Big Dogs

Today the bridge crossing the Wind River from downtown Dubois leads to a subdivision. In the '1940s and '50s the Boedeckers were the only town residents who used that bridge to get home. They had two big dogs guarding their house. Because of the tie hacks, my grandfather said.

The hardiness of the tie hacks is well known. From 1914 onward they felled trees in Union Pass and Towgwotee Pass, then skillfully "hacked" them into railroad ties. In the spring they floated the ties down the Wind River, breaking up dangerous jams along the way. At the treatment plant in Riverton the ties were infused with creosote and delivered to the Chicago & Northwestern.

Today we understand what the tie hacks did during working hours, but we know little about how they spent their time off ... except that many drank. The Wyoming Tie and Timber Company did not allow the camp commissary to stock booze. But vanilla extract sold well. So did dried fruit. Various concoctions could be fermented, then distilled using a pressure cooker and copper tubing.

But that was in the winter, when deep drifts isolated the men high in the mountains. After the snow melted tie hacks headed into Dubois on weekends, where drinks could be purchased at the bar and consumed at the gambling tables.

My grandfather recounted a Saturday night when a group of tie hacks started back to camp late. Their Model T ran off the road and into a deep borrow pit, scattering drunks as it bounced down the embankment. The men gathered around the car, lifted it, and carried it up the steep slope to the road. Someone turned the crank. They were on their way again.

Many years later a few retired tie hacks still lived in Dubois. Saturday nights they would go to the bar and afterward, feeling old stirrings, might set out for the large house standing by itself on the other side of the river. That's why the Boedeckers still had to keep guard dogs, even though they had bought the place from the woman who owned it years before.

Many of the Dubois area tie hacks had been recruited as young men from isolated logging camps in Scandinavia. After suffering sea sickness, seeing more strangers than they knew existed, and traveling more miles than they could comprehend, they again found themselves secure in an isolated logging camp among men like themselves who spoke a familiar language.

There was a puzzlement though. Many wondered about the pigmentation of two fellow workers who were American born. People with African genes were another new experience for the young Swedes. According to my grandfather, the older tie hacks would remain silent until a wide eyed newcomer finally asked. Then they'd say, "Oh, you mean Bill and Jim? We all start looking like them after a few years here."

4 *Amorettis, Father and Son*

Pete and Eleanor Ridgeway, my uncle and aunt, lived their last decades on Amoretti Street in Lander, two blocks south of Eugene Street. Both streets were named for the "Father of Lander," Eugene Amoretti Sr (1817 – 1910). His son, Eugene Jr, appeared in an earlier story as Butch Cassidy's employer, my grandfather's employer, and my almost employer.

Amoretti Sr was one of those 19th century gentlemen who set out from Europe for the New World hoping to enrich themselves. Some had aristocratic, even royal, pretentions. Some were but a stride or two ahead of pauper hood, a condition many never escaped. Amoretti, however, succeeded extravagantly.

After wandering in South and Central America, Amoretti turned up in California for the gold rush of 1849. Grasping a truth of gold rushes—that selling shovels is a surer way to riches than digging holes—he prospered. When he arrived in Wyoming for the South Pass gold rush in the late 1860s, he was able to invest in several mercantile operations and buy several promising mines.

While Amoretti was getting richer at South Pass, two communities were engaged in fierce competition 30 miles to the north at the foot of the Wind River range. Both were lobbying to be chosen as the site of the post office.

One candidate, Push Root, was located on land that had been homesteaded by Benjamin Franklin Lowe. As yet a modest community, it consisted principally of a hotel and livery stable operated by Peter Dickinson.

The other applicant was North Fork, five miles north of Push Root. It was a thriving collection of saloons and brothels that met the social needs of the cavalry troopers stationed at Fort Washakie. Amoretti had a store there too.

In 1875 Push Root was awarded the post office on condition it come up with a respectable name. Today we know it as Lander.

The loser, North Fork, was subsequently renamed Milford. When I was a teenager the passing years had reduced Milford to two buildings, a small store and a barn converted to a dance hall. Its heritage endured, however. My cousin Jim Ridgeway and I used to attend cowboy dances there, some rowdy.

In subsequent decades Amoretti created not only the town of Lander but much of the early economic infrastructure of northwestern Wyoming.

His son, Eugene Amoretti Jr, joined him in many of those ventures and launched projects of his own. As a teenager he founded the EA Ranch north of Dubois. After Twogotee Pass was opened to motor traffic, Amoretti Jr founded a transportation service that carried tourist from the railhead in Lander to Moran, in Jackson Hole, where they could connect to motor stages that came down from Yellowstone. For that project he built the Brooks Lake Lodge and the Amoretti Inn, the predecessor to today's Jackson Lake Lodge.

5 *You Knew People Who Knew People Born 200 Years Ago*

Eugene Amoretti Sr, the "Father of Lander," was born more than 200 years ago, in 1817. He died in

1910. I never met him, of course. But I knew someone who did know him, and well: his daughter in law Francis Amoretti. in 1950 Mrs Amoretti was my employer when I worked on the EA Ranch near Dubois as a 13 year old chore boy. She was approximately the age I am now.

Mrs Amoretti was acquainted with Amoretti Sr. I was acquainted with Mrs Amoretti. Therefore . . . when I was young I knew someone who knew someone who was alive in 1817; that is, two centuries before today.

Many of us Depression babies, now long in the tooth, in our youth knew older persons who knew someone who was born in the early 1800s. As an almost universal experience perhaps, some older folks in every generation remember people who remembered people who were born 200 years before their present time.

Or to put it another way, only two memory links connect me and my generation with someone who was alive in 1817—me to Mrs Amoretti, and Mrs Amoretti to her father in law.

Prior to his death in 1910, Amoretti himself likely remembered from his youth an older person who knew someone who was born 200 years earlier. That is, around 1720.

That would add two more memory links—for a total of only four memory links—between you and me today and someone who was born well back in Colonial times, more than six decades before the colonies declared their independence from England. One more memory link, a fifth, would take us all the way back to the founding of Jamestown.

We communicate little and forget much. From generation to generation most of our personal memories are lost, despite the surprisingly few links that connect people across history.

6 *Helping Build the Teton Theatre*

The Teton Theatre in Jackson opened in 1941. I helped build it.

The stone mason from Idaho who was in charge of the project sometimes hired me as his helper. My job was to pound rock fragments for him. I was three years old. He paid me a penny a shift.

I have a strong tactile memory of sitting in the dust in shorts and sandals, hammer in hand, looking at a half dozen stones with an intense sense of purpose.

The stone mason was a good friend of my mother and stepfather. They were drinking with him the rainy night he turned away from the bar, walked out the back door to take a pee in the alley, and was found later—having passed out, fly open, face down in a shallow puddle—drowned near the building he was constructing.

7 *Hank Boedeker, Lawman*

Google Earth shows a log residence in Dubois on the southeast corner of Mercantile and Clendenning Streets. Mom, Little Mike (the bartender at the Rustic Pine and her purported husband at the time) and I lived in that house the year I turned 14. Barbara and I drove by several years ago. It had that dark, time-stained patina of an old log house, just as it already had 70 years ago.

Google Earth also shows a newer street curving up the hill to a recent development east of town. Its name is Boedeker Street.

A nice gesture, I thought, for the Town to name a street after "Bump" Boedeker (pronounced Bedeker, 1899 - 1980). For years Dubois depended on Bump. He drove for my grandfather's truck company and hauled the mail and freight from Riverton five days a week.

Perhaps 80-90% of the food and small goods that were bought, sold, and consumed in Dubois came in on Bump's truck—as well as the movie the whole town attended every Sunday night in the dance hall at the Rustic Pine Tavern.

Recently I was informed that Boedeker Street was not named for Bump after all. It was named for Hank, Bump's father; just as Boedeker Butte on the T-Cross Ranch had been a century earlier.

Hank Boedeker (Harold, 1859-1947) arrived in Wyoming via Illinois and Nebraska in 1883, eventually settling in the Dubois area. He was a larger than life Wild West hero. As a lawman his historical reputation was enhanced by a coincidence: Hank shared the Wind River country with Butch Cassidy in the early 1890s.

One story, almost certainly true, reports that as town marshal in Lander Hank was among the party that escorted Cassidy to Ft. Laramie to serve a prison sentence. He had been convicted of stealing thirteen horses near Meteetsee. A trumped up charge, some historians claim. (Which raises an existential question. If a man is a for sure criminal, has an injustice been done if he's sent to jail for a crime he didn't commit?)

According to another story, Cassidy and his gang rode into Lander one day and were confronted by Hank, who asked them to surrender their guns for the duration of their visit. The others complied, reluctantly and only because Cassidy agreed. Cassidy agreed only because of his close personal connections with the E.A. Amoretti family, owners of the Amoretti Bank—and much of the rest of Lander as well.

That story gratifies but is likely not true. No evidence has turned up of a "Cassidy gang" frequenting the Lander area.

On the other hand . . . it is true that Cassidy and a partner, Al Heiner, operated a horse ranch on Horse Creek upstream from Dubois. And it's reasonably certain that not all the horses they sold had been acquired legally. Reportedly people commented at the time that Cassidy and Heiner maintained a good inventory, regardless how many customers rode away on new mounts. (Another apocryphal story maybe.)

And we do know that Cassidy visited Lander often, and it's likely that Heiner was with him on some occasions. But when a pair of horse thieves rides into town, their effect isn't the same as a gang of bank robbers.

8 *Watkins Lakes, Part of the Family History*

Times change, losses occur, the heart remembers. Around 1950 an event happened that ruined a cherished tradition—our family's annual camping trip into the Watkins Lakes.

The Watkins Lakes are a pair of small lakes in the shadow of the Ram's Horn Peaks. Our family's connection with them began in the early 1900s, when my grandfather was growing up in Dubois. The connection was still firm when I was a kid in the late 1940s.

Three generations of us had renewed that bond every summer. My boyhood memories include driving up Dunoir Creek, going through a gate into the National Forest, fording a strong flowing creek, then driving what seemed a long way through the timber on a rough dirt track. Eventually we'd arrive at a pretty little meadow where a spring bubbled out of the hillside.

We'd camp there for a few days, hiking the mile or two over a hill to fish in the lakes. Around the fire in the evening the grownups would retell the family's Watkins Lakes stories.

Back in the 30s, for instance, they returned from the lakes carrying the day's catch of brook trout. As they approached camp they heard clanging and banging, ripping and tearing. They watched from a distance as a big grizzly marauded through their camp. Suddenly the grizzly roared. It took off for the timber, snarling at every step. When the camp was being put back in order someone found a bar of soap—rather, half a bar of soap—gouged by big teeth. The other half had gone up the mountain mashed up in the mouth of the enraged bear.

The adults also told about the night my young life almost ended in that meadow. We slept communally on the floor of a big wall tent. In the dark I untied the lowest tie holding the tent flaps, crawled out, and peed. As I crawled back in I was suddenly blinded by a light. Uncle Pete, flashlight in one hand and length of firewood in the other, was poised to club me. He thought I was a bear.

The pickup hauling our camp got stuck in the creek one summer. Grandpa and Uncle Pete started attaching a pair of come-alongs to trees, intending to winch the truck out by hand, inch by inch. Then a man showed up in a Jeep, a vehicle relatively unknown to civilians at the time. He crossed the creek, turned around, drove back in, and hooked onto the front bumper of the truck.

He told Uncle Pete to put the pickup in neutral and just steer. Then he put the Jeep in reverse. Unassisted, the Jeep pulled the heavily loaded truck across the creek and up the steep gravel bank onto level ground.

My Grandfather, who had spent his life operating heavy equipment, watched thoughtfully. Within a week of returning to Riverton we had a Jeep of our own parked in the driveway.
That Jeep never made the Watkins Lakes trip

though. Something bad happened …

9 *History Riles People Sometimes*

When I posted the following story about the Watkins Lakes on the Wyoming Early History Facebook group, it drew many responses, and mixed ones. Some people were angry. A few accused me of supporting fence-cutting trespassers driving recreation vehicles.

That wasn't my intention at all. I write about what happened. About how people thought and felt when I was growing up decades ago, and about the things they did then. Occasionally I write about how things have changed since. I write about history, in other words.

Fence-cutting trespassers driving recreation vehicles are part of today's history, not the history of the Wyoming when I was growing up in 75 years ago. Then we had different notions of land stewardship and community. Bad intentions determined whether crossing another person's line constituted trespassing, not so much the act itself.

People entered other people's rural property unthreatened, but with respect. Folks talked with each other, got acquainted. And putting up No

Trespassing signs was considered unfriendly citified behavior, plain bad manners in fact.

Here's the story that stirred feelings . . .

10 *Big Money Started Buying Wyoming*

Bad news came down from Dubois one spring day in the early 50s. New people had bought the ranch where the Dunoir Creek road ended—then the only road into that part of Shoshone National Forest and the Watkins Lakes country. The new ranch owners had padlocked the gate into the national forest.

(A disclaimer: That was a long time ago, I was a boy, and today's map is much changed. It shows several roads and trails into the area that did not exist then. I don't remember which ranch was involved or who owned it then, nor does it matter now.)

The local uproar was loud. People demanded the Forest Service enforce the public's right of access. A meeting was called. The new owners sounded accommodating. They had no intention of locking local people out of the National Forest, they said. They only wanted to make sure the gate stayed closed so their cows wouldn't wander. (Wyoming people don't leave gates open. But we understood their concern.)

They said we were welcome to stop by the ranch and get a key to the gate. (Well. Okay.)

The owners also asked that we unlock the gate, then drive back to the ranch and return the key before proceeding. (A pain in the butt. But kind of made sense.) And they asked that we not leave the gate unlocked behind us when we continued on. (Of course not.)

Soon folks in Dubois, and the Forest Service authorities, realized they had been slicked, maybe deliberately, maybe not. The new owners of the ranch had in effect sequestered thousands of acres of public lands to their own use. And they didn't do it by locking people out, but by locking people in.

When we entered the Watkin's Lakes country in accordance with the owner's rules, we had a long wait at the gate when we came back out. Someone had to climb the fence, walk the two miles to the ranch, ask for the key, then walk back.

Going to the Watkins Lakes wasn't fun anymore. Folks came home mad.

11 *About Shooting People*

This sign is planted beside a road in the Dubois area (or used to be in recent years).

NO TRESPASSING

Trespassers will be shot.

Survivors will be prosecuted.

It occurred to me that some people today may believe the sign speaks in the manly pioneer voice of Old Wyoming. To me, however, it speaks in a new, mean, angry voice that's often heard in Wyoming nowadays.

Some people were uncomfortable when I once expressed that opinion on Facebook. A few defended the message on the sign. They said the landowners were properly affirming their rights. Others said I shouldn't take the sign literally. That it was just, well, a joke. That no one actually intended to kill anybody.

The thing is, I understand that. I believe that if my car broke down, Wyoming is still a place where outsiders can safely flag down a ranch vehicle and ask for help. The assistance would be extended, and in a hospitable and generous spirit, just like seven decades ago.

On the other hand, 70 years ago no one was stock-piling military weapons with large capacity magazines and declaring their readiness to kill fellow Americans over political differences. Threats to shoot people can't be jokes anymore.

When I was growing up we had guns and were taught to use them. Lesson #1 was: Never shoot anybody. Roy Rogers never shot anybody, nor did Gene Autry. Eventually John Wayne started shooting people, as did **Charlton Heston**, Clint Eastwood, those guys.

But movie heroes kill people wisely and justly. The directors and script writers always make sure of that. The hero shoots only bad guys, for good reason, at the right time and under the right circumstances. To make sure we understood the situation correctly when we were kids growing up, the bad guys always wore black hats. My uncle Pete used to call those fantasies "horse shit and gun smoke movies."

But John Wayne and Clint Eastwood never actually hurt anyone. They weren't even allowed live ammunition on the set. They were just actors pretending to make the world right by killing people.

12 Fifty-five Below Zero. The Stove Blows Up

On the list of coldest days ever recorded in Wyoming, February 1, 1951, ranks fourth. The temperature in Dubois fell to 55 degrees below zero. That was the night the oil heater blew up.

As some will remember . . .

Back in the days when people were converting their homes from wood (or coal) to oil heating, many chimneys were well suited to the new arrangement. The old houses had been built around a centrally located stove pipe or chimney. T-fittings opened into other rooms so wood heaters could be connected.

Besides the obvious advantage—a single chimney for multiple fires—the system was energy efficient. As the stove pipe or chimney passed up through the house, it radiated heat from the stoves below. Some rooms didn't even need a fire except on the coldest nights.

That advantage continued after the wood burning heaters were removed and a single oil heater was installed downstairs. The old chimneys still carried heat directly to the rooms above.

When the wood burners were taken out, the open T in each room had to be closed off. Welty's store sold closure plates, made of tin, that snapped in.

The plates had pretty pictures on them . . . floral arrangements, noble stags, pretty girls waving ribbons while cavorting with lambs, that sort of thing.

The frigid night of Feb. 1, 1951, I was sleeping upstairs at a friend's house. The oil heater had been blasting away on its highest setting all day. When we went to bed it was making strange sounds—hums, moans, groans.

Just before midnight . . . BOOM.

The later diagnosis: following the conversion to oil, oily soot had been building up inside the stove pipe, constricting it. Under the heavy load that night, superheated fuel was backing up into the stove's combustion chamber. BOOM.

The explosion did no direct damage. But it jarred loose all that oily soot that had accumulated in the stove pipe. Simultaneously it popped out the closure plate in every room. In an instant, the whole house and everything in it changed color.

I was 14. When I went to basketball practice that day, my long underwear was grey. When I took it off I was pale white from the neck down and from the wrists up, with a sharp line between.

13 The Mystery of the Dubois Cave

Today I'm passing on the definitive answers (according to my grandfather) to three questions people in Dubois have been asking for a long time. Who dug the cave, when, and why?

Dubois has not always been a town divided. In the early 1900s most buildings were located east of the ridge that runs parallel to Horse Creek and splits Dubois from the north.

That ridge terminates in a sandstone bluff just a few steps from Main Street. A conspicuous man-made cave was dug into the rock there at a time beyond remembering.

When I was a kid in Dubois in 1950, the cave was still closed by a locked grill bolted to the stone. Both the grill and padlock, long gone today, were crusted with rust. No one seemed to know why the cave was locked or what it had been used for, nor who dug it or for what reason.

I understand that local authorities have made several attempts, over the decades, to promote a back story that would interest tourists: a gold mine, a jail, and, more mundanely, a cold storage place are just three I've heard about. Some people have even claimed the cave was "Butch Cassidy's hideout." Not likely though. Cassidy wouldn't have hidden in a place where everyone on Main Street could see him.

None of those suggestions are true. Back in the 1950s Cody Simonson, my grandfather, told me the story.

He said his father built a saloon in Dubois around 1900. It was located immediately west of the ridge on the site that later became the Branding Iron Bar. He said his father (my great grandfather) discovered he could not secure his whiskey stock in a wooden building, not one that was out of sight on the outskirts of town. His back room was broken into regularly.

The sandstone bluff stood handy, next door to his bar, in full view of Main Street. He hired miners to blast a cave into the soft rock, stacked his cases of whiskey inside, and locked them behind an iron gate.

14 *Union Pass, 1955, Something Ends*

In 1955 John Raymond and I decided to celebrate our graduation from Riverton High School by exploring the Union Pass country. The Warm Springs Creek Road from the highway west of Dubois ended at Lake of the Woods. A few rough tracks branched out from there, four wheel drive only.

The area was quiet in those days. The tie hacks were gone. The only people there were a ranch couple who for years had been operating a summer cow camp out of a cabin at Lake of the Woods. They were folks my grandfather had grown up with in Dubois. We took in fresh fruit and vegetables for them. They provided us with the unexpected comfort of a wall tent with a floor and wood stove.

The only others we ran into were Pete Peters and his family, roughing it on vacation. Pete was the Wyoming Highway Patrolman for Fremont County. John and I had never seen him out of uniform before, or unshaven for a week.

It was a great trip. We fly fished for arctic grayling Game and Fish had stocked in Lake of the Woods. We fried up a dumb grouse. (Dumb because she allowed me to get close enough to shoot her through the head with my .22 pistol.) We investigated the old wooden chute the tie hacks used to float logs down the side wall of Warm Springs Canyon.

Earlier, planning how we'd get around in the mountains had been no problem. We'd just take my Jeep. (It wasn't really my Jeep. The registration said it belonged to my Grandfather. But he hadn't driven it since the day I got my license four years before.)

On the other hand, deciding how best to get the

Jeep to the mountains had taken some thought. It was one of the older models . . . hard seats and 45 miles an hour on the highway. My grandfather had welded a tow bar to the front bumper, but John and I didn't have anything to pull the Jeep with.

Then John found a good buy on a trailer hitch. It was attached to a big Packard, about the same age we were, with a straight 8 engine. The Packard ran well, though it got about the same mileage from a quart of oil as from a tank of gas. It didn't go far on a tank of gas either.

Some young men from a place far to the east of Wyoming had been on a road trip. When the Packard's battery died in Riverton, they were broke and stranded. John bought the car from them for $50.

Then he didn't have enough money to buy a battery either.

Undaunted, we hitched the two vehicles together and headed for the mountains. We rode the highway in comfort, the Packard pulling the Jeep by the tow bar. We started the Packard easily, pushing it by the tow bar with the Jeep.

Over the years John and I had explored many places in Fremont County together. But our lives took different directions after Union Pass. We had only one more trip together in that old Jeep, hunting mule deer in the Owl Creek Mountains.

A Very Young Man
In Riverton

PHOTO. In 1954 Riverton High School was represented at the Wyoming State Track Meet by a six man team. At the conference championships we had qualified to compete in four State events. We won gold medals in all four and took third place overall. From left: Don Ricks, discus; Jay Chrisler, LeRoy Sinner, Clarence Whipple, and Jim Bishop, 440 relay; Jim also won the 100 yard dash; Ray Laue, mile. *(Riverton Ranger)*

1 *I'd Never Been in a Brothel Before*

Pete Peters and I always waved when we met on the highway. He would be in uniform at the wheel of his Wyoming Highway Patrol cruiser. I would be driving a semi for the Barnes Truck Co., the family business.

The minimum age for a license to drive commercial vehicles was 18. I was 16. Pete knew that. People in Fremont County got along together in those days. They believed in keeping things in perspective.

Consider prostitution for example, a business model Wyoming State Law frowned upon. On impulse I pulled off the highway one morning and parked my truck next to a big rig with Casper plates. I was about to commit an act of teenage curiosity and bravado. I had never been in a whore house.

Known as the Blue Goose, the blocky two story building stood alone outside Shoshoni. The sign conveniently declared it a CAFE. I ordered pie and coffee.

I was surprised, first of all, by the demur attractiveness of the woman who took my order. She'd be a strong candidate for Miss Fremont County. Wearing light makeup and shower fresh, her shapeliness implied under a crisp waitress uniform, she was the girl next door. I was expecting lipstick and rouge, suggestive clothing, blatant marketing.

I was also unprepared for the ease with which business was conducted. When the Casper truck driver finished his ham and eggs and drained his coffee cup, the waitress asked in a quiet voice, "Do you want to go upstairs?" He nodded. They went upstairs. Surely arranging sex with a woman you didn't even know had to be more complicated than that.

Another woman, older and plainer, appeared from the kitchen and refilled my cup. Just some folks making a living showing other folks a good time.

2 *Soldier Comes Home, Breaks the Law*

When WW2 ended 1st Lt. Max Crowe, my father, returned to Wyoming wearing decorations for wounds and acts of courage. He also brought home a marketable skill. He could make a blackjack deck or pair of dice do just about anything he wanted. (Provided they were his deck and his dice.)

We saw each other occasionally during my teens, though he moved around. Someone told me he was running a table in the basement of a club in Shoshoni. (Yes, Shoshoni again, that small town den of iniquity.) The person gave me directions for finding him.

Gambling was against the law in Wyoming. A more dramatic narration might report that a secret entrance opened onto stairs leading down to a casino. I'll make do with an inconspicuous door in the service area between the bar and the dining room.

A blackjack table and a craps table crowded the windowless room. My father, his partner and I weren't alone for long. It was Friday evening, payday. A tall young cowboy came down the stairs. As I hoped, he headed for the craps table. I already knew how Max's blackjack deck worked. I wanted to see a croupier stick in action.

The cowboy won a few rolls, then lost. He won a

few more, then lost. After a while he was losing about four times for every three wins. Eventually he held up his hands, said good naturedly, "I'm cleaned out," and climbed the stairs.

The croupier complained. "I've got to stop wearing these damn tight saddle pants." Reaching into both pockets, he pulled out two hands full of matches, keys, coins . . . and dice. "I had a hell of a time changing dice on him."

I had watched closely. Nothing touched the dice on the table except the croupier's stick and the cowboy's hand. It's been more than sixty years now and I still haven't figured out how a croupier stick works.

Fremont County authorities didn't share the State's negative attitude toward gambling. They considered my dad and his partner just a couple of guys working the weekend so other folks could enjoy leisure activities. Both provided a service to the community, like those ladies at the Blue Goose out by the highway.

3   *Gerry Spence Saves Fremont County from Sin*

One morning in Riverton Gerry Spence was seen nailing flyers to utility poles: Spence for County

Attorney. Today Spence is well known in Wyoming and across the nation. He is the lawyer who, almost singlehandedly, created the multi-million $ judgments routinely awarded in civil litigation cases.

Now the little guys can finally get a fair shake against the big guys. Or, litigation is so costly now that juries have to award big bucks to make sure plaintiffs have something left after the lawyers get paid. Depends on a person's point of view.

But that is now. In his autobiography, The Making of a Country Lawyer, Spence admits that then he wasn't much interested in being Fremont County's attorney. The pay was regular though. A recent graduate of the University of Wyoming Law School, a little brash by local standards, his new practice was not prospering.

Spence promised that, if elected, he would clean up gambling and prostitution, both thriving businesses in the county despite being illegal under state law. Gambling and prostitution were topics seldom discussed except at election time, when they predictably turned up in candidates' platforms. Most people understood the pledges weren't intended to be taken literally.

Spence also did something unprecedented and considered politically outrageous. He went onto the Wind River Indian Reservation and asked the people of the Shoshone and Arapaho tribes for their vote. He won the election.

Spence promptly set to work trying to get rid of gambling and prostitution. He says those who ran Fremont County would have none of it. They believed people like themselves, community leaders in business and politics, should not meddle in each other's leisure activities.

The sheriff assured him that anyone charged would not be arrested. The judges assured him that anyone arrested would not be convicted. Everyone assured him that no witnesses were going to testify they had ever been upstairs in the Blue Goose. Others objected too. For instance, the person who passed Spence on the highway one night and put a bullet through his car window.

Nevertheless, Spence cleaned up gambling and prostitution, in short order and quietly. He says he sent a deputy to stake out the Blue Goose and record license plates. He matched those cars to their owners. He then put out word that he intended to call a grand jury and would subpoena names on that list. On the other hand he promised, the whole issue would just disappear if the county started enforcing the applicable laws.

The gamblers and prostitutes departed from Fremont County. My father Max Crowe, a blackjack dealer with big but dexterous hands, was among the gamblers who left. The next time I tracked him down, 25 years later, he was managing a sheep ranch near Ten Sleep.

❖ ❖ ❖

4 *Spence and I Had Different Perspectives*

Gerry Spence and I both visited the Blue Goose, though neither of us went upstairs. As a curious teenager I stopped at the CAFÉ for pie and coffee. He went in his official capacity as prosecuting attorney. In his book he reports coarse behavior, "powdered cheeks and bright red painted mouths." In my version I reported "demure attractiveness . . . light makeup and shower fresh . . . the girl next door." We must have stopped at the Blue Goose on different days.

❖ ❖ ❖

5 *Willa Wales Corbitt Paves Riverton*

There was a time, as people left Shoshoni, they could see where Riverton was located. It was under that big cloud of dust off to the west. Except for a few primary streets, Riverton was not paved. On the side streets cars and trucks drove on gravel. And raised dust.

Riverton's streets could not be paved for two reasons. First, Riverton couldn't afford to pave its streets. That's what everyone said.

Second, oil and water don't mix. That's what everyone said.

What they meant was . . . pavement and irrigation don't mix. When a town does not have sidewalks and concrete curbs running alongside its streets, but has community irrigation ditches instead, it's stuck with gravel. The streets of Riverton could not be paved because people depended on the irrigation ditches flowing in front of their houses for watering their lawns and gardens.

"Nonsense," said Willa Wales Corbitt. "We're going to pave the streets."

"Nonsense yourself," many said.

But not everybody. Certainly not those of us who, as students at Riverton High School, had taken Algebra from Mrs Corbitt. Or Geometry. Or Calculus. We knew that if Mrs Corbitt said something was nonsense, it was nonsense. And if she decreed the streets of Riverton were going to be paved, they would be paved.

"So how is this miracle going to happen?" the doubters asked.

"I'm going to run for mayor," she answered.

She ran; she won. She passed a bond issue. She filled most of the irrigation ditches and replaced them with sidewalks and curbing. And she paved the streets.

People in Riverton started watering their lawns and gardens by hose. And they no longer lived inside a tan haze all summer.

Riverton's soft-water artesian wells began pumping dry years sooner than anyone predicted, but that's a different matter.

6 *Finding the Birdseye*

"Sergeant Ricks."

"Sir?"

"Wind River Canyon is blocked by a rockslide. Do you know the old stagecoach road to Thermopolis through Birdseye Pass?"

"Yes Sir."

"Take a duce-and-a-half. Take Sergeant Raymond with you. Hurry."

"We're on our way Sir."

I'd never driven to Thermopolis via the Birdseye

Pass road. I'd never even heard of Birdseye Pass, in fact. But I did know where, north of Shoshoni, a dirt road left highway 20 and headed in the general direction of Thermopolis, an unknown distance away. Seemed worth a shot. There weren't nearly as many roads as today, and a commanding officer confronting a crisis wants a decisive solution, not a nuanced explanation.

John Raymond and I had shared adventures before. We'd been exploring wild areas of Fremont County since the day, shortly after I turned 15, my grandfather loaned me the keys to his Jeep and never saw them again. Now we served together in the Wyoming National Guard, Battery C, 349th Field Artillery Battalion, Armored.

By 1913 the Burlington Northern tracks had been dynamited through Wind River Canyon, instantly putting out of business the stagecoaches that used the Birdseye. The pass continued as a motor route, passable in fair weather with fingers crossed, until the early 1920s, when the highway was opened through Wind River canyon. Since then . . . who knew?

Parts of the rough track challenged even our Army truck, with its high clearance and six wheel drive. The eroded, seldom used road had not been maintained for decades. But Thermopolis eventually came into sight, as promised and to my relief.

Lt. Andrews would never have to know that I'd just

driven the Birdseye Pass road for the first time.

◆ ◆ ◆

7 *How Lt. Andrews' Butt Gets Saved*

Sgts. Ricks and Raymond, driving a Wyoming National Guard 6 X 6 truck, made a rough, hurried trip on the old stagecoach route through Birdseye Pass, as Lt. Andrews had ordered.

They were concerned when they arrived in Thermopolis. It was Saturday. The bottling plant would probably be closed. They didn't know how to contact the manager to complete their mission . . . which was to return to Riverton with a truck load of soft drinks.

Battery C, the Riverton National Guard unit, was sponsoring an air show at the airport that day. The contract stipulated the gate receipts would be split between the Show and the Battery—after the Show had collected a guaranteed amount. If the gate receipts didn't cover the guarantee, the Battery's concession receipts would have to go into the pot. Any further shortfall had to be covered personally by those who had signed the contract. That was Lt. Andrews, the commanding officer, and his executive officer.

That guarantee to the Show began to cast a dark

shadow as the date approached. Someone pointed out that, because air shows are performed in the air, people could park in the sagebrush outside the airport fence and watch the stunts for free. There might not be any gate receipts.

Then, on the eve of the event, a rockslide in Wind River Canyon blocked the route from the bottling plant in Thermopolis. The concession profits were in doubt too.

So a worried Lt. Andrews sent Sgts. Ricks and Raymond to Thermopolis to bring back a load of pop. Sending them via the old stage coach road through Birdseye Pass was a desperate move, and a long shot.

The two young non-coms made it to Thermopolis as ordered and returned to the airport by the time expected. But their truck was empty.

Business was booming at the airport when they got back. A sizable crowd was milling inside the fence examining the stunt planes and the display of military equipment. A long line of cars was backed up at the entrance gate, waiting to pay the entrance fee. The air show was making money.

The concessions were raking in cash too. The battery cooks had fired up the field kitchen and were selling hamburgers and hotdogs. Under the hot August sun, people were lining up to buy soft drinks too. The drinks were chilling in galvanized watering troughs filled with ice.

Though the two young sergeants had failed to complete their mission, the day had been saved. The hero turned out to be the bottling plant manager in Thermopolis. Having his own financial stake in the event, he had called the Wyoming Highway Patrol. The Highway Patrol agreed to allow his truck through the slide area on the rough track being used by the road clearing machines.

When the cavalry rode up in a 6 X 6 half an hour later, a patrolman waved them around the long line of waiting civilians too.

◆ ◆ ◆

8 *Brawling in the Bar at the Wort*

I was required to submit old time credentials to join the Facebook group, Jackson Hole in Simpler Times. My list included a fist fight in the Wort Hotel bar when I was 19. Here's how that happened.

Four young men, wearing the hat, and the boots, and the big belt buckle, were being loud and unruly. A young couple, conspicuously eastern and likely on their honeymoon, was passing through the bar on their way to the dining room. As the couple walked by, one of the cowboys reached out and touched the woman inappropriately.

She said Eek. Her husband said What happened? The cowboy said Wanna fight?

I stepped forward and said something to the cowboy; something that seemed appropriate, given the circumstances. One thing led to another.

9 *Uranium! We're All Going to Get Rich*

In the mid 50s Wyoming uranium boom was, well, booming. According to a story making the rounds, a local opportunist we'll call Gary met a mark in a bar in Riverton. The mark was a wannabe millionaire newly arrived in town with a pocket full of cash and an itch to own his own uranium mine.

Gary just happened to have a very good claim for sale. And he could explain convincingly the circumstances that forced him to part with it for ready cash now and forgo becoming a millionaire later. The two men agreed to meet for breakfast, then go look at the claim.

Gary, according to the story, drove into the desert that night, planted a 4' X 4' post in the ground, and the next morning sold it to the mark for $50,000.

The story is likely apocryphal. But it just might have been true because of a smaller-than-a-breadbox device called a Geiger counter . . . and because of uranium's little secret.

The Geiger counter made prospecting a totally new endeavor. A man could get out of his pickup, turn on his machine, and start walking through the sagebrush. He was prospecting. If his machine started clicking with sufficient excitement, he had found uranium.

And uranium's secret? It is a relatively common, widely distributed mineral in much of Wyoming. Thirty-five million years ago it was deposited in scattered beds of ash spewn from the earth by volcanic eruptions in the Absaroka Range; that is, in the Yellowstone Park area. And, thanks to the Geiger counter, uranium is easy to locate.

In the '50s knowledgeable prospectors were searching for an elusive find: uranium deposited in concentrations sufficient to be profitably mined. Others were filing claims on "hot spots" all over the place.

So the scam story sounds more plausible if we assume Gary planted his post in a location he already knew would tickle a Geiger counter. That morning the mark could have flipped a switch, heard chirps, and believed he was going to be a rich man.

The uranium boom brought a lot of money into Wyoming. And while a few opportunists like "Gary" may have been around, the boom did create many legitimate ways for locals to prosper. The next story is about my first entrepreneurial venture. At age 17 I went into business selling my services as a validator of uranium claims.

◆ ◆ ◆

10 Getting Rich at 17

The summer of 1954 the uranium exploration boom was peaking. More than 7,000 claims would ultimately be registered in Fremont County alone, in blocks of 20, 50, 100 or more. Many Wyoming folks were making a good living providing services and supplies to the invasion of prospectors. Some locals stayed with their day jobs while running lucrative businesses on the side.

I was between my junior and senior years in high school and wanted a break from hauling drilling mud for the family truck company. Wages were good, a buck fifty an hour. There was plenty of work. So I freelanced as a laborer. I helped roof a house; painted the interior of the Sky Club, a new (and short lived) supper club in the basement at the Riverton airport; and then I got a job making holes in the ground.

A uranium claim would expire in a year unless the claimant filed a statement, signed by a validator, declaring the validator had performed mineral exploration work sufficient to meet BLM requirements. One way to validate a claim was to drill along the centerline. Multiple holes would serve, as long as each hole was at least 10 feet deep and the total added up to 100 feet. The holes didn't have to turn up signs of uranium. They just had to be drilled. And they didn't come cheap.

I was hired, along with a 14 year old helper, to validate claims with a small auger rig that made a 4 inch diameter hole. It was mounted on the back of a Jeep pickup and had a seven-foot mast. Theoretically the little rig could drill to 100 feet. But it had several limitations. Bedrock would stop it instantly, of course. Or a seam of wet, heavy clay would try to suck the whole rig down the hole. We occasionally validated a claim with a couple of 50 footers; were pleased when we needed to drill only four 25s; and sometimes had to settle for ten 10s.

A small camping trailer was provided so my helper and I didn't have to drive back and forth to town. We were paid by the claim and validated an average of four claims a day. That is . . . when we had claims to validate. Our boss's real business was operating a supper club in Hudson. Spending most of his day behind the bar, he didn't find enough work to keep us busy.

My entrepreneurial instincts kicked in. I found out that Bob Burleson, a Riverton pharmacist whose real business was running a drug store, was brokering claim validation contracts as a sideline. I negotiated a hand shake lease of the rig with the club owner. Then I subcontracted with Bob to fulfill his drilling contracts and paid the rig owner a percentage.

I replaced the young helper with a friend my age. We streamlined our drilling procedures to model the efficient operations we had seen on oil rigs. Soon I was signing off on ten claims a day, twelve if the drilling was easy. My helper was averaging $50 a day, I was banking $125, and the supper club owner and the pharmacist were happily making more than both of us combined.

Then football practice started and I had to go back to high school.

◆ ◆ ◆

11 *Dark Night, Dark Shapes*

My Grandfather shook my shoulder. "Wake up . . . You have to go to Gillette." There was urgency in his voice. The tool pusher who phoned in the order said the drilling crew at Gillette was waiting.

A 600 mile road trip in the company pickup, paid by the hour, with an overnight stop in a new community, should have been a welcome assignment for a 17 year old. But it was Sunday morning. I'd slept for only two hours and had barely started to sober up.

As instructed, at a rig south of Riverton I picked up a bit sub (a 250 pound extension to the drill string) and drove to Casper. In Casper a welder was waiting, having agreed to open his shop on Sunday for the emergency repair.

By late afternoon I was headed north on Highway 220, still urged on by the need to hurry. A big thermos of coffee lay on the seat. It had been topped up twice since my Grandmother filled it early that morning before I left.

In Gillette I checked into a motel, ate, and got directions to the rig. By 11:00 I was driving through the sage brush on a gravel road.

Something big, dark, and unfamiliar loomed in my headlights. Then two additional shapes appeared, then more. I stopped the truck. Through my caffeine induced fog, I realized I was surrounded by buffalo. Only three or four small herds existed in Wyoming at the time.

At the rig I climbed the steps to the dog house expecting a hero's welcome. "I'm finally here." The Driller seemed puzzled. "I've brought your bit sub from Riverton."

"Oh, yeah, that." He went out and looked down into the back of my truck. Um . . . just toss it on the ground over there."

Regarding those buffalo . . . I lived a mobile life while growing up in Wyoming. But those were the first open range buffalo I'd ever seen.

◆ ◆ ◆

12 *Got the Gun, but What's the Plan?*

It's 3:30. That's a.m. I'm finishing my ham and eggs at the only all night café in Laramie. And I'm wondering. "I'll go out and start the car. Then what'll I do?" Returning to the dorm and going back to bed seemed the most sensible alternative.

The whole idea seemed pretty straightforward in the beginning.

This was in 1955. I had enrolled as a freshman at the University of Wyoming on a football scholarship a few weeks earlier. Everything was going well except for a knot of discontent, deep inside and growing. Deer season was coming. Deer hunting in the fall, like playing football, was built into my circadian rhythms. Both were something I always did when the leaves turned. I had assumed skipping it that year would be painless, but it wasn't.

What seemed the biggest impediment between me and going deer hunting was easily solved. Cordon

Barnes, my grandfather's partner, was coming to Laramie for the annual meeting of the Wyoming Truckers Association. He brought my .270 from Riverton.

Bought a deer license; read the regulations for the area; sharpened my skinning knife; gassed up the car; set the alarm clock . . . was ready to go hunting.

Now, sitting in that café in the wee hours, I had to confront a major decision that could be deferred no longer. Where would I go? Where exactly would I look for these deer I intended to hunt? Except for Laramie and the highway that got me there, I knew nothing about that part of Wyoming.

A plan began to take shape as I headed west toward the Snowy Range. Once well out of the city, at every intersection I took the least traveled road. Soon I left pavement behind. A few choices later I was no longer on gravel. I was following a pair of dirt tracks in the grass.

Just as the sun peeked over the ridge—that is, the moment hunting season opened—I pulled up at a small creek, got out of the car, loaded my rifle, and walked into the cottonwoods. Minutes later I was dressing out a fat spike mule deer. I was back in Laramie by 8:30.

Solutions continued to turn up as I needed them.

What does a freshman living in a dorm do with a

dead deer? Well, attached to the back of the Athletic Dorm I found an empty stone shed once intended for landscaping tools. I skinned the deer and left it hanging there. The fall days remained cool.

So a week later what does a freshman do with 100 pounds of prime deer meat, properly aged? Well, the other guys in the dorm and I got together and sliced the deer into steaks.

The couple who cooked for the Athletic Dorm had an entire half day off every week. After serving the noon meal on Sunday, they left sandwich makings for us in the big fridge and went home.

That evening we jocks fired up the grill and ate venison instead of bologna.

13 *Two Weeks Was Long Enough at Camp Guernsey*

Camp Guernsey Wyoming, June 1953, a Saturday. The work day has just started. A dozen of us are gathered in the battery headquarters tent. The officers are wearing khakis. The enlisted men are wearing fatigues; they all have stripes on their sleeves.

Except for me. My fatigues don't even hang right

yet. Recruited barely three months ago, I'm a big 17 year old who is standing in awe. And in apprehension. Before the meeting is over an issue is going to be raised . . . something I'd rather not try to explain.

The 349th Field Artillery Battalion of the Wyoming National Guard has finished its summer maneuvers, and Battery C is getting ready to return home to Riverton. The residents of the Guernsey area won't miss us. We're a noisy bunch. Machine guns, both 30 and 50 caliber; bazookas; various small arms; and especially those 155 mm howitzers that make a sharp bang, followed by a loud boom miles away.

The battery leadership has gathered to plan a quick getaway the next morning. Everyone's a little homesick.

Several decisions are made. The cooks will serve a cold breakfast with hot coffee, and a KP crew has been assigned to help them clean up and finish loading their kitchen trucks. All the other trucks will be loaded and lined up in the battery street by the end of today.

Nothing will remain standing in the battery area except two big sleeping tents jammed wall to wall with cots. The tent stakes are three feet long. Today every second one will be pulled to save time taking down those tents in the morning.

That was a decision we regretted later. When everything was loaded and ready to go, we all headed for the PX to celebrate the end of summer camp. We were well launched on our mission to assure no beer got left behind at Camp Guernsey when a big wind blew in. We had to stagger out to rescue the tents.

The preparations for an early start completed, Lt. Andrews issues his departure orders. At 0645 every trooper must be settled in his assigned vehicle and every driver have his engine started. The command jeep will lead the convoy through the camp gate at 0700. We'll be on our way home to Riverton.

This is the moment I've been dreading. Lt. Andrews scans the gathering. "Private Ricks?"

All eyes are on me.

14 *Told the Lieutenant What He Could Do with His Jeep*

My previous post ended at Camp Guernsey in the headquarters tent of Battery C, 349th Field Artillery Battalion, Wyoming National Guard. Our 1953 summer maneuvers over, the brass and stripes have just finished planning a quick getaway the next morning. Now everyone is thinking about the trip home.

This is the moment that's been worrying Private Ricks, a new recruit, 17 years old.

I'm at the meeting only because I'm the prime mover driver. In military terms, a prime mover is whatever vehicle is being used at the time to tow an artillery piece.

During the two weeks in the field at Camp Guernsey, I've been driving a tracked armored vehicle as my prime mover. Tomorrow, back on the highway, I'll again be pulling the 155 mm howitzer with a 2½ ton 6 X 6. At almost 13,000 pounds, the howitzer is a heavy haul for a deuce and a half. (Yes, *the* howitzer. The battery, understaffed at the time, barely qualified for one. Three years later we would be issued a second howitzer, self-propelled.)

Two weeks previously, at 0700, the command jeep had led the battery vehicles out of the parking lot at the Riverton Armory. My truck, the one pulling the howitzer, was relegated to the rear of the convoy (as the Standing Order of March decreed). Camp Guernsey was 231 miles away.

We arrived much later than scheduled. The troopers were still unloading trucks after dark.

And my name was being mentioned frequently. Everyone thought I was a bad driver. The other

drivers had to keep slowing down to let the howitzer catch up.

They didn't understand. Following behind the convoy as it accordioned up and down the long hills
between Riverton and Casper, I was never free to
build up speed on the downhill runs. I always had
to shift into low gears on the uphill grades.

As the meeting begins to wrap up, Lt. Andrews
issues his departure orders for tomorrow at 0700.
Then he turns to me, as does everyone else in the
headquarters tent.

"Private Ricks."

"Sir?"

"It took us eleven hours to get here from Riverton.
Can we make better time going home?"

"Yes sir."

"How, Private Ricks?"

"Put the howitzer behind the lead jeep Sir."

An image of the lead jeep formed in my mind. The
jeep would be setting the mandated speed for the
convoy—45 mph. The First Sergeant would be at
the wheel. The Commanding Officer would be in
the passenger seat. Private Ricks would be looking
down from the cab of the truck immediately behind, frustrated.

I hesitated. Then I blurted out: "And tell whoever's in the lead jeep to stay the hell out of my way on the downhill runs . . . Sir."

Battery C pulled into the Riverton Armory early the next afternoon.

❖ ❖ ❖

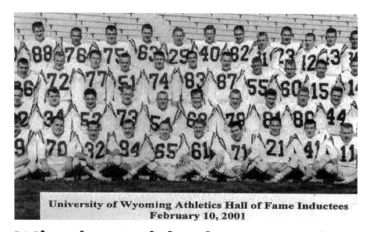

University of Wyoming Athletics Hall of Fame Inductees
February 10, 2001

Winning With The Wyoming Cowboys In 1956

PHOTO. The 1956 University of Wyoming football team. Out-scoring our opponents 252 to 112, we beat every team we played and ended the season ranked 16th in the nation. Having trained at 7,200 feet, we owned the fourth quarter. #74, center of photo, is me.

1 *How I Became Ricks from Riverton*

For years afterward newly met Wyomingites would say, "Don Ricks? You're from Riverton, right?" The name recognition was puzzling.

True, I had played football for the Wyoming Cowboys, and on a memorable team, undefeated and nationally ranked. But my role was nearly anonymous. I was an interior lineman and played only that one season, as a sophomore.

My promotion from fourth string had been a last-minute act of coaching desperation; a more experienced player cracked his sternum bumping while warming up for the first game of the season. I did play in all 10 games, and in almost all 40 quarters. But that was inevitable because complicated substitution rules, eventually rescinded, forced coaches to go three deep every period.

Yet people seemed to have heard of me. Eventually a former athletic department insider revealed a conspiracy.

As many will remember, Larry Burleffi, the radio announcer, was known as the Voice of the Cowboys for forty years. Some may also remember that Roy Peck, publisher of The Riverton Ranger, served on the University Board of Trustees in the 1950s.

After a board meeting Roy reportedly took Larry aside to make two requests. When broadcasting football games Larry should say "Ricks" at every opportunity. And whenever he said "Ricks" he should say "from Riverton."

So that football season "Ricks from Riverton" was broadcast throughout the State of Wyoming every Saturday afternoon at least eight times. The four times the coach sent me into the game. And the four times he took me out. Alliteration took over from there.

2   *Ricks from RHS Lines up Against Heroes*

In the spring of 1955 I received a letter from Phil Dickens, head coach of the Wyoming Cowboys, offering me a football scholarship. I accepted by return mail.

Except for offers to a few players within the state, Wyoming was not an easy sell for recruiters. It was a long way from home for most high school athletes and had only recently become competitive in the NCAA. The coaches scoured the country, especially the East, the South, and the military teams. (Remember the movie Mash?)

The athletic department seemed to offer scholarships to any promising freshman who would agree to come to Laramie. The coaches stuffed the third floor of the athletic dorm to twice its capacity, two double bunks in every two person room. Our class started out with 55 freshmen on full scholarship.

Then the coaching staff set out to determine who was worth keeping. Practice sessions—strenuous, demanding, sometimes ferocious—were designed to take our measure and hasten our maturation. Those of us still standing when September came again would have a shot at playing for the Cowboys as sophomores.

When we freshmen reported in, the varsity players were already in their second week of twice a day practice. Wednesday we began working out in sweat suits. Friday after practice we were issued pads. The Saturday scrimmage pitted the freshmen against the varsity.

So there I am in defensive stance—Ricks from Riverton High School. In the backfield of the opposing squad I see heroes. Joe Mastrogiovanni. George Galuska. Jim Crawford. All three will be NFL draftees. One is a future first team All American, another honorable mention. I'm wondering which of them is about to carry the ball and whether I'm defending the hole he intends to run through.

The opposing linemen are heroes to me as well, including Vince Guinta. He will be honorable mention All American at center—twice. Previously I had admired those guys from afar on Saturdays. Now we are down in playing position face to face, separated by the length of the football. Someone over there intends to knock me on my butt.

On Monday following that first scrimmage, only 43 freshmen showed up for practice. Of the initial 55 recruits, a dozen had turned in their pads. They'd already experienced enough football as it was played at the University of Wyoming.

A year later eight of us took the field every Saturday against Cowboys opponents. Not all of us were the most talented athletes in the recruiting class. But we sure were a stubborn bunch.

3 *The Whistle Game*

Interviewed afterwards, every game official denies blowing his whistle.

No Denver player hears a whistle. No Denver fan

hears a whistle.

Every player in a Wyoming uniform—and every Wyoming fan in the stadium—hears a whistle. Even I hear a whistle, and I'm a freshman at home for Thankgiving listening to Larry Birleffi on the radio.

It's November 25, 1955. Wyoming vs. Denver at Denver. Fourth quarter, the score is 0 – 0, and time has almost expired. Joe Mastrogiovanni kicks a 17 yard field goal. Wyoming 3 – Denver 0. Ten seconds left on the clock.

Wyoming kicks off and Denver sets up a hook-and-ladder. After several laterals succeed, the Denver ball carrier disappears under a mob of Cowboy tacklers. At the exact moment everyone in the stadium either hears a whistle or doesn't hear a whistle, the ball pops out of the pile, is snatched from the air by a Denver player, and ends up in the end zone. The game's over. Denver has won, 6 - 3.

Both benches clear. The officials and coaches are on the field breaking up fights.

The event goes down in Wyoming Cowboys history as The Whistle Game.

4 Going Both Ways

Dave Rupp played offensive guard on one of the Cowboys' greatest teams ever, the 1966 version. I played tackle on a lesser but undefeated team ten years earlier.

During an exchange of comments following one of my posts, Dave declared me among "the last of the Iron Men." He remembered our team as part of the final generation of college football players who went both ways, playing offence and defense too. I wrote back, "Damn right we were Iron Men."

Then I had to confess. We Cowboys—like all of college football from 1953 - 1963—were ensnared in the dumbest NCAA rule ever written.

Some people, with who knows what influence, had decided that football was played "the right way" back in leather helmet days, when everyone on the team had to be an all- around athlete. They invented a complicated substitution rule intended to ensure players played both ways. We all had to show up on Saturday ready to play offense. And defense. And special teams. Just like in high school. Only worse.

Coaches could not substitute freely. Field goals? Punts? An extra point attempt, then a kickoff? The kicking had to be shared among the players who happened to be on the field at the time. A lineman might drop back to block for his team's kick returner; then, if his team scored or ran out of downs before his shift was finished, he'd run down the field intend on tackling the other team's kick returner.

Fresh squads didn't always run onto the field when the ball changed hands. The players already there just changed alignments. The players who had been playing offense became defenders. The linemen still played in the line. Except for the center. The center and the fullback became the linebackers. The wingback and the tailback became what are now corner backs. The quarterback was the safely.

Here's how the substitution rule worked. At the beginning of each quarter, a coach handed one of the officials a list of the players who would start. Those eleven players could play for a shift, be taken out of the game, then could individually be sent back in during the quarter. But only once. Nonstarters could be sent into the game only a single time. When the coach took them out, they were no longer members of the team for the duration of that quarter. They warmed the bench along with any starters who had played twice.

See. Nothing complicated about it at all.

Recently I found online the films of two of our games from six decades ago. I was gratified to see that on offense I was a reasonably effective blocker.

Wouldn't win many style points certainly. But in those two games at least, no Cowboys ball carrier was tackled by a defender I was assigned to block.

On the other hand, those films also demonstrated that nature had intended me to be a defensive tackle.

5 *Turning Green Freshmen into Green Shirts*

When we newly recruited freshmen reported to the Cowboys in August, 1955, our introduction to college football was abrupt. We worked out in sweat suits for three days. Then on Saturday we put on pads for the first time and scrimmaged the varsity. Twelve freshmen packed their bags that weekend and went back where they came from.

Three weeks later Phil Dickens, the head coach, called the whole team together at the end of practice. He scolded us freshmen for disrupting workouts. He said we were picking too many fights with the varsity. That had to stop.

All along John Townsend, who coached the freshman team, had been insisting we fight. He demanded belligerent aggressiveness, even when we were lined up against players who were second and third year starters. We liked Coach Dickens' idea better.

Looking back, I believe Dickens instigated the brawling behind the scenes, then intervened publicly to shut it down when it had accomplished two objectives. More recruits, disheartened by the violence, had been culled from the team. And although those of us who remained were still freshmen, we were no longer kids just out of high school.

We had become the Green Shirts. Every week that season we learned the basic playbook of a new team. Our job at practices was to play aggressive football against the varsity in the style of their next opponent. The Cowboys won 7 of 10 games. We helped them get ready for the Sun Bowl. They beat Texas Tech 21-14.

Back at the start of the season, 55 of us had arrived as freshmen on scholarship. When spring practice began in April, 25 of were still on campus. The following August, 12 reported as sophomores. That season 8 of us lettered on an undefeated, nationally ranked Cowboy team.

6 Why We Didn't Get a Bowl Bid

How come the Wyoming Cowboy's didn't get a bowl invitation in 1956? We were undefeated and nationally ranked. For years people asked me that question.

There's a familiar answer that used to give some comfort. The Cowboys did receive a bowl initiation. But we turned it down because we hoped for a better one. That is the true, but not the whole story. The real story is ugly. Coach Phil Dickens totally screwed up our hard won bowl opportunity to play in a bowl game. I'm about to disclose what used to be a dark Wyoming Cowboys secret.

Getting into a bowl was tough in those days. There were only seven bowl games: Cotton, Orange, Rose, Sugar, Sun, Tangerine, and Gator. That's 14 invitations across the nation. By comparison, in the 2017/18 season 80 teams got bowl invitations.

Nevertheless, we did get invited to a bowl. The Cowboys had won the previous Sun Bowl. As our season was winding down, the Sun Bowl committee sent a back channel message. . . if the Cowboys would agree to accept an offer, we would receive one. We were welcome to play in the Sun Bowl again. They said they understood, though, that we were probably hoping for a more prestigious invitation.

We were on the Gator Bowl short list. The coaching staff thirsted to take us there. Dickens announced that we players could vote on the Sun Bowl offer. The way he put the matter came out as, "If you want to pass up your once in a lifetime chance to play in the Gator Bowl and just go back to the Sun Bowl again, raise your hand."

Walking away from the Sun Bowl invitation was not Dickens' big blunder, however. He had weighed our chances of getting a Gator Bowl bid, made a decision, gambled, and lost. Fair enough.

His huge dereliction was that, even though he'd put all his chips on the table, Dickens himself didn't play out the regular season. He neglected to coach us for our final game, against BYU. Too busy preparing for the Gator Bowl maybe.

After beating Montana, our ninth win, we turned out for practice on Monday. Dickens announced we'd had a spectacular season and earned ourselves an easy week. We'd just have light workouts.

Dickens failed to consider that the BYU team, 0 – 9, could, in a single game, redeem their entire losing season. They just had to defeat undefeated Wyoming. The BYU players certainly wouldn't have an easy week. They'd be working their butts off. And it was going to be a home game for them. The BYU student body, known for hazing visiting teams, would be driving themselves into a frenzy of support.

When we got off the bus in Provo, we lacked our accustomed pregame edge. We'd barely practiced our own game, knew little of BYU's game, knew nothing about their individual players. Worst of all, we were emotionally flat and nonmotivated. Dicken's game plan: Show up and win again, as you usually do.

Nevertheless, we did beat lowly BYU, rescuing our undefeated season. The final score was 7 – 6, with them barely missing a field goal in the closing minutes. The Gator Bowl representatives didn't see us win the game by one point though. They walked out at half time.

Dickens acknowledged his mistake and apologized. We players have lived our lives as members of a championship Wyoming Cowboys team that should have played in a bowl game but didn't.

7 *Why Game Preparation Matters*

Every football game is different. Every player experiences playing differently. Some of our Wyoming Cowboy games seemed to me to be played in slow motion. Every step, every movement, the opponents' and mine both, seemed almost leisurely, deliberate. Other games seemed to be played beyond full speed. The ball would be snapped—three to five seconds would flash by—and a whistle would blow. I might be 20 or 30 yards from where the center snapped the ball, with maybe a new bruise or two.

The perceived velocity of a game didn't seem to matter for some reason. I experienced the same situational awareness, the same reactivity and body control, at either speed.

That was because of the game preparation the coaches designed for us. And, for me at least, because of private preparation rituals.

John Townsend, the assistant line coach, never attended a Cowboy game that season. He was always in some other city scouting our coming week's opponent. Teams around the country shared game films as well.

So each week we were exposed to plenty of information about the team we were going to play on Saturday. Some kinds of knowledge might be useful to one player, different kinds to another. For me information about the upcoming was interesting but not playable.

The important preparation for me came on the practice field after the coaches had turned the scouting information into live drills. The equipment manager would dig into storage and bring out an old set of jerseys that matched, approximately at least, the color our opponents would be wearing. He also matched as nearly as he could the numbers the opponent's best players would wear.

Meanwhile, the assistant coaches would be studying films and diagramming the opponent's plays. Then the green shirts would put on those jerseys and run those plays against us, repeatedly.

During practice drills we would react to images similar to the ones we'd see on Saturday. I didn't exactly learn from those drills. It was more like I imprinted. I acquired reactions to the other team's offensive patterns at a level beyond conscious awareness.

I self-prepared too. No one had yet invented the term bio-feedback, but I used it every week. Wednesday evening I would deliberately give my system a squirt of adrenaline. My dose Thursday evening was three squirts. Friday night, usually while studying, I would deliberately raise my adrenaline level a bit at a time, then keep myself charged up.

However, during our final game that season I played emotionally flat and lead footed against BYU, as did the rest of the team. Coach Dickens and his staff had neglected to prepare us for the game. I lined up against their offense without any imprinted reactions to focus my defensive play.

I didn't play well against Montana the preceding week either. My private Friday night rituals were disrupted. Dennis Krueger, a personal friend and superb all around athlete from Cody, came to Billings to watch the game. The Wyoming coaching staff thirsted to recruit him. Dickens instructed me to spend the evening with Dennis. "Go to a movie or something." On Saturday I didn't have "my mojo" as they say now. Montana scored one of its two touchdowns on a long run right through my position. I misread the pattern of the play and went around a blocker instead of through him.

8 *Coaches Had Strange Beliefs Then*

Football coaches believed in yelling at players back in the '50s. (I understand some still do.) They believed players should not be coddled. We were supposed to be tough. Therefore they held to certain disbeliefs, disbeliefs that puzzle sports professionals today.

Coaches did not believe in face protection, for example. Joe Mastrogiovonni, a player from Brooklyn with a marvelous Italian schnauz, suffered multiple nose fractures. The athletic department finally sent him to Denver for plastic surgery. (He came back with a pointy little beak.) Then the coaches relented and protected Joe's face—with a single bar across his helmet between nose and mouth.

When we reported for my sophomore season the next fall, we were surprised to find all our helmets equipped with the same simple bar. The coaches explained their concern. The Athletic Department was spending too much money on dental bills.

Coaches did not believe in hydration either, either during games or during three hour practices. We sucked lemon slices to quench our thirst. The coaches said we would get stomach cramps if we drank water during heavy exertion. They must have been right. We were denied water and nobody ever suffered from stomach cramps. Players did go down with muscle cramps though.

Most puzzling, football coaches didn't believe in giving players positive feedback. They used praise avoidance instead.

9 *Coaching with Praise Avoidance*

In the 1950s, when I played for the University of Wyoming, football coaches berated players, frequently and loudly. They didn't believe in giving players positive feedback either.

Coaches preferred praise avoidance as a coaching technique. Here follows a report (the long version) about how a Cowboys line coach once used praise avoidance to develop a young tackle—with apparent success.

The previous season the Cowboys had won the 1955/56 Sun Bowl, beating Texas Tech 21-14 after being down 7-14 in the fourth quarter. During the following summer the pundits were uncertain when announcing their preseason predictions. Wyoming looked strong again, the prognosticators said, except at tackle.

Though the sports writers didn't know it yet, the team was loaded with experience at strong side tackle, my position. Grown men who had played while serving in the military lined up on the first, second, and third strings. (Two untried sophomores, a guy from Ohio and I, anonymously shared the fourth/fifth strings.)

The day came for our first game. A lineman was injured during warmups. Minutes before the opening whistle of my first varsity season, I was suddenly promoted to third string tackle.

Bob Hicks, the line coach, was as surprised as I was. The complicated substitution rules in force at that time required him to send three players into a game at every position during every quarter. And those players had to play offense, defense, and special teams. He had to play me in that game, and possibly later ones as well, whether he considered me ready for NCAA competition or not.

Here's how Coach Hicks responded to the unexpected challenge of developing a young tackle quickly—using praise avoidance.

Monday following that opening game, my first film night ever, I was deeply absorbed in what was happening on the screen. I had never watched myself play football before. Sitting in that darkened room surrounded by teammates, I was learning something every play.

Suddenly Coach Hicks' voice boomed out. "Ricks, they let you through on this next play." Then I watched myself sack the Western State quarterback. I was confused by the coach's accusatory tone. Did I do something wrong?

During film night after our second game, against Arizona, I watched myself sack the quarterback. "Ricks, they let you through again."

The film of our third game showed me sacking the Denver quarterback. Silence.
I noticed, however, that for the rest of the season Coach Hicks often sent me into the game in passing situations.

I do remember a film night compliment. "Good block by the strong side tackle. Is that you

Hauser?" "No sir. That's Ricks."

10 *Ricks, have you been drinking?*

One Saturday night in 1956, halfway through Cowboy spring practice, the assistant football coaches posted themselves at the entrances to the Athletic Dorm, clipboards in hand. They had come to enforce the training rules. All football players were supposed to be in their rooms at midnight, sober.

At 11:59 I walked into the dorm. Bob Hicks, the line coach, intercepted me. "Ricks, have you been drinking?" His nose was inches from mine, checking for the smell of alcohol on my breath.

I exhaled "No . . . Sir."

"Go to your room and go to bed."

At practice Monday anxiety was in the air. The coaches had said nothing. Not yet, anyway. The players were exchanging questioning glances. "You get caught?" "Yeah. You too?" "Yeah."

The practice was long, strenuous, and ended the usual way, with all of us sucking air following repeated hundred yard wind sprints. Instead of sending us to the showers, the coaches signaled us to gather round. Ass chewing time had arrived, we thought.

The coaches stood silent, expressionless. We waited. Coach Hicks stepped forward, paused, then looked down at his clipboard. "When your name is called, start running laps."

"Zowada. Ginta. Watts. Crawford, Jim. Crawford, Jerry. Houser. Tolson. Allan. Memmelarr. Finch . . . The list continued . . . Murratore, Benson. Mireski. McGill. Marshall, Bob. Marshall, Hank. Stapleton. Maushart. . . . ."

Eventually Coach Hicks lowered his clipboard. "Everyone else . . . hit the showers."

The other guy's name was Hansen. He was from Newcastle, if I remember correctly. He and I turned away and started jogging toward the field house. We showered, dressed, and when we walked out of the building, the rest of the team was still on the track.

11 *The Day We Made Jim Crawford an All American*

In 1956 Utah State (Utah A&M then) fielded the biggest opponent I ever lined up against. Fortunately for us, that was four years before the great Merlin Olson's time. Olson played at 270. That guy in 1956 weighed in at 340. He would have outweighed Olson by 70 pounds, and did outweigh me by 145 pounds. But unlike Merlin, he never became an NFL All Star.

Nowadays in college football 340 pound tackles are uncommon but not rare. The USU heavyweight was not a modern day 340 pounder, however. Football teams didn't have weight rooms then. And coaches didn't believe in lifting anyway. Several myths circulated regarding what weightlifting "really did" to an athlete's muscles. USU's big lineman had just put away a lot of groceries.

We tackles on the Cowboy team couldn't move him out of the hole. But we could make sure he didn't go anywhere else. Our running backs blew by him a yard on either side. I went low and drove my helmet between his knees, hoping he didn't fall on me when he tripped. On defense I was past him almost before his knuckles left the ground.

That was a good day for the Cowboys. We had growing aspirations for an undefeated season.

Also, Jim Crawford was ranked first in the nation at running back and was a candidate for All American. But Jack Hill, Utah State's running back, was ranked a close second. He was also leading scorer in the nation. He kicked field goals and extra points as well as scoring touchdowns.

So we ran onto the field with two objectives and achieved both. We won the game, 21 - 0. And our defense held Hill to 17 yards and scoreless. Jim ran for 132 yards. At the end of the season he was named All American running back, first team.

A decade later I visited Logan a second time—for a job interview. As a faculty member in the English Department at Utah State, I became an Aggie fan for four years. Except for every other year, when the Cowboys came to town.

12 *My Teammates Cheer Me on Film Night*

I recently found an old sports page article online that reported a play I remember. I also remember what happened afterwards, during film night on Monday.

We were playing Utah State at Logan. On this particular play, Larry Zowada called a reverse. John Watts, our All Conference wingback, would run the ball. John and I were lined up on the right side of the formation. When the ball was snapped John ran to the left, took a handoff from Larry, and ran wide around the left end. My assignment was to make a pretense of blocking the defender in my zone, then take off diagonally across the field to intercept John and block downfield.

Now . . . I was a tackle who was faster than most tackles. But I wasn't faster than any wing backs, especially John. John was the Skyline Conference 440 champion and the fastest man on our team.

The design of the play gave me a shortcut angle to get into the action, but only if I ran, you know, really really fast. I arrived just ahead of John. Aspiring to throw a touchdown block, I turned up field, targeted the defensive safety, and kept running full out, hoping John wouldn't run up my back.

When that play came up on the screen Monday night, Coach Hicks' voice boomed out. "Ricks, block somebody." Right on cue and to the cheers of my teammates, I tripped over my own feet and sprawled face first in the grass.

The play gained 31 yards and set up a touchdown, according to that old newspaper clipping.

13 My Best 60 Seconds of Football

Two old black and white game films have turned up online from our 1956 Cowboys season. One contains a memorable five minute segment. During those five minutes I decided I was playing on an undefeatable team; saw that judgment confirmed; and played my personal best 60 seconds of football ever.

Having won our first six games, we were facing Kansas State at home. They were punishing to play against. Many were big, rangy farm boys. Wyoming could move the ball. The Cowboys ran for more than 220 yards that day, with Jim Crawford getting 175 of them. And Larry Zowada racked up 140 yards on just three of his passes alone. But scoring was tough. In the third quarter they stopped us three times inside their 20.

We came out for the fourth quarter fired up. Kansas State had the ball and was leading 6 – 9. On the third play of the quarter they scored on a long breakaway run, one of those touchdowns that, late in a hard fought game, can break the spirit of a defense. We were trailing 6 – 15 and still hadn't cracked their shell.

I scanned our team. There was no defeat in

anybody's eyes. Nobody was sitting on the bench staring at the ground. The team's silent but unanimous consensus was clear. The Cowboys had decided to win the game. K State's fourth quarter touchdown just meant we needed to score an additional touchdown of our own. That's when I realized I was playing on a championship team.

That five minute film segment shows what happened next.

The Cowboys received the kickoff and the squad in the game started driving down the field. Four minutes later Wyoming had closed the score to 13 – 15.

After the kickoff I was among the players sent in. On our second play on defense, K State ran an option play my way. My defensive assignment against the option was to prevent the quarterback from running the ball. I was supposed to either tackle him or force him to lateral. The end, linebacker, and cornerback would gang up on the halfback going wide.

I hit the quarterback squarely just as he started to lateral. The ball jarred loose on their 20 yard line. Buster Elder, our end, recovered the fumble.

We lined up in offensive formation. I made an adequate retaining block on the guard while Jim Crawford picked up five yards outside on a sweep. Then Zowada called the most powerful play in football—off tackle to the strong side of the single wing formation. Jim would run through my position.

My assignment was to block the defensive guard, who would be lined up on my nose or inside shoulder. To my right our end and wing back would double team the defensive tackle while Zowada and the fullback double teamed the defensive end.

But K State had called a strange defensive alignment. Or maybe someone just made a mistake. No lineman was defending my blocking zone. The Cowboy guard to my left called out, "Zone loaded, Don." That meant he would not be pulling to lead the play through the hole. He had to stay to block the defensive guard lined up on his inside shoulder.

So the hole was wide open. No one was in set position between Jim Crawford and the goal line except me and the K State linebacker, who was now my blocking assignment. I blew out the linebacker and Jim scored untouched from the 15 yard line.

That put the Cowboys ahead, 20 – 15. In a minute and four seconds we had scored 14 points and taken the lead. We won the game 27 – 15. We won the rest of our games as well.

14 *My Bright Shining Moment as a Wyoming Cowboy*

Many of us old jocks remember a bright shining moment, a single event of our youth that affirmed our finest realization of ourselves as athletes. Looking back more than six decades . . .

As a 196 pound sophomore, I played third string tackle for the undefeated Wyoming Cowboys in 1956. An acquaintance told me about something special that happened. It occurred after the season ended and far from where I was at the time. Without his report, I would never have known.

Coach Phil Dickens was making the traditional round of post season appearances at Quarterback Clubs across the state. In Rocksprings someone quoted a truism—"You can't win with sophomores"—then asked Dickens how he managed to go undefeated even though he played eight sophomores in his regular rotation.

Dickens answered by going down the list, recounting the football history of each sophomore. Seven were older and more experienced than the seniors on the team. Grown men in their mid twenties, they had played in high school, then three or four years in the military, before receiving a scholarship at the University of Wyoming.

"Then there's Don Ricks from Riverton," Coach

Dickens reportedly said. "Don is a true sophomore, 19 years old. But he's the only player on our team who never makes the same mistake twice."

I did make all the mistakes once, of course. But Coach Dickens didn't mention that.

15 *Why I Quit Football*

After lettering as a sophomore, I gave up my Wyoming Cowboy football scholarship. The decision was surprisingly easy. I had plenty of excuses.

Playing on another undefeated, nationally ranked team was unlikely, especially with a new system coming in. (Devaney had replaced Dickens, who had gone to the Big 10.) I would never be selected All Anything. Still having two years of eligibility, I might aspire to start; but 196 pound tackles were not in great demand. My academic load was getting heavier as I started taking more advanced courses.

Those were my rationalizations in 1957. Half a lifetime later I discovered, within myself, the true reason I was so ready to quit football that spring. That spark of self-knowledge flashed when I happened to remember a sports moment in high school.

Cheney was among my opponents at the track meet that day. I don't mean Lynne Cheney of course. She and I did attend the same grade school in Casper for a few months. But she was just a little kid and not even a Cheney yet. Dick was a little kid at some other school in Casper at that time; nobody had heard of him.

I'm speaking of Tom Cheney, Dick's older cousin, a star athlete in Worland later, when I was in high school.

By my junior year two events could be predicted at track meets in the Big Horn Basin. Dennis Krueger, an exceptional athlete from Cody, would easily take gold in the discus; I would take silver. (Except for the year Dennis came down with the mumps and I ended up state champion.) In the shotput Dennis would win unchallenged; Tom Cheyne would always take second; I would place a close third.

Then in my senior year I got well into the shot at the conference championships. My distance turned out to be a new RHS record. I was so elated by the feel and distance of the throw I barely noticed when an official planted my marker in second place.

Tom noticed. He shouldered me aside as I stepped out of the ring, set himself quickly, and determinedly made his own best put ever, taking back second place. Tom, being a Cheney, competed to win, to defeat his opponent.

I understand now I've always been a self-competitor. The contest is between me and the game, not me and the opponent. Even years later in my forties, when I was playing city league basketball against twenty somethings, at the final buzzer I often didn't know which team had won until I looked at the score board.

My objective at the track meet that day was to put that 12 pound ball farther than I ever had before. I achieved that goal. But I still placed third behind Tom Cheney.

When I enrolled at Laramie in 1955, my athletic goal was to make the Wyoming Cowboys football team, an awesome aspiration for a high school kid from Riverton. By the spring of 1957 that goal had been achieved, sooner and on a larger stage than anyone would have predicted.

Meanwhile, the self-competitive high school athlete had been morphing into a self-competitive university student. New goals beckoned; new energies were required. It was time to leave football behind.

Finding My Father In WW2

PHOTO. Lt. Max Crowe knew these men and went to war with them. Notice the unit designation on the Jeep's bumper, 104 R. The 104th Recon Squadron was Max's unit. Flying American and Soviet flags, this patrol led by a Lt. Shank (likely second from left) was the first 104th Division unit to contact the Russians on the Elbe, at Pretsch.

1 *In Search of My Father*

The Wyoming kid grew up. I'm in my 80s now. For years one of my disappointments in life (besides never learning to play the classical guitar) was that I didn't sit down with my father and a tape recorder, then write a book that preserved for posterity his account of World War Two.

When recounting his war experiences Max was not always factual, however. Having researched his stories, I know that now. So let me begin by declaring that my dad, 1ˢᵗ Lt. Max Crowe from Riverton, Wyoming, was an honest to goodness hero of World War Two. As a researcher I found nothing in the historical documentation that casts doubt on his valor or the integrity of his service to his country.

Yet there are two versions of Max's war. He told one version over the years in the Big Horn Bar in Ten Sleep. He often repeated those same narratives at other times and places with friends and family. That's the version of Max's war I grew up knowing; and often retold to others in later years; and wished I had written for him.

The second version does not always agree with the first. It's the version that emerged when I began researching the historical documents in the family scrapbook. Some claims Max made about the war were proven accurate. Some were found to be questionable. And some turned out to be outright whoppers.

But in the coming pages those stories won't be dwelt upon. Max was a raconteur. His stories served his purpose at the times and places he told them. There's no point now in quibbling about this one or that one or refuting any of them.

While I will set the record straight occasionally, my main intention is to recount and celebrate the truths of Max's war, and truths of the man himself. Both are worthy of remembrance.

What follows are not simply war stories. They are also stories about how a soldier's son—who grew up to be an historian—gradually reconstructed his father's war by researching papers and photos in the family scrapbook, and by researching other sources those documents guided him to. I then determined where the live events revealed in the documents fit into the larger context of the known history of the war.

Incidentally, I claim to be an historian because the departments of English and History both signed off on my research degree. Maybe I'm only half a historian. But perhaps that's enough for present purposes.

◆ ◆ ◆

2 Lt. Max Crowe's War

Here are the barebone facts of the historical version of Max's war. He was called up with his horse cavalry regiment of the Wyoming National Guard even before the war started; and he was not discharged until the war ended five years later. He spent most of the war in Oregon training with the newly formed 104th Infantry Division. The division was shipped directly to France in August, 1944.

In late October the 104th division was moved up to the Belgium/Dutch border in preparation for the Battle of the Scheldt. On October 29, 1944, Lt. Max Crowe experienced combat for the first time—and immediately proved to be good at it.

During the subsequent 200 days, Max led a platoon of the 104th Reconnaissance Squadron (Mechanized) from the Dutch border almost to the Elbe during the Allies' relentless advance across Germany. He was decorated twice for valor, was wounded more than once, and spent three weeks in a German POW camp. I'm proud to recount my father's war exploits for today's generations.

3 *Lt. Max Crowe, War Raconteur*

Max told an expanded version of his war, one that cannot be substantiated historically. Being a raconteur, he was more interested in his audience than his story. He spoke to entertain people and hold their attention, not to teach them history lessons. Many of Max's stories were essentially true, if not entirely. All were told well and convincingly.

My research did expose outright falsehoods. But often Max just told good a tale and allowed people to hear what they wanted to hear. A person listening to Max could easily get the impression he was involved in far more fighting than he actually experienced, from the very beginning of the war and in places he'd never been.

He didn't claim he fought in the Aleutians for instance, or in North Africa, or Sicily, or Normandy. On the other hand, he never said he didn't fight in those places. He told stories about those campaigns in a manner that created an impression of personal experience—"The Germans really whipped our butts there"—even when he was recounting only generally known historical episodes.

Max was an easy person to like, an easy person to believe. He was a muscular, handsome, blue collar gentleman, quiet, differential, self-effacing. People still write to say how much they liked and admired him. So it's easy to understand why his friends in the Big Horn Bar christened him "the most decorated man from Wyoming in World War Two." (A claim he himself never made, according to people who were there.)

We should also keep in mind that during the years when the 104th division was training in Oregon, Max was acquiring a non-military vocation after hours. Following the war he returned to Wyoming a skilled professional gambler. He could make a blackjack deck, or a pair of dice, do whatever he wanted (as long as they were his deck and his dice). Gamblers, like magicians, are experts at distraction; they are adept at making people trust what they think they saw and believe what they think they heard.

The stories you're about to read constitute the researched version of Lt. Max Crowe's war. It is an historically accurate account, as nearly as I could make it. It reveals worthy service by a brave young soldier from Wyoming.

Initially ten source documents were available in the family scrapbook: two bronze star citations; three V-Mail letters written by Max; a first person account, written after Max's death by one of his sergeants, of his capture by the Germans; a laudatory letter about Max signed by Major General Terry de la Mesa Allen; and three clippings from The Riverton Review written when Max returned home as the war was winding down. Following up on those sources led to the discovery of more sources—and to some unexpected surprises and insights.

First, the first bronze star citation.

4 *Max Gets Shot At, Shoots Back*

The family scrap book contains two bronze star citations. Max was awarded the first one for acts of heroism he performed on October 29, 1944, his very first day of combat.

> BRONZE STAR MEDAL—CITATION
> ". . . In connection with military operations in Holland on 29 October 1944 . . . Lieutenant Crowe's platoon encountered an enemy road block covered by artillery and small arms fire. In spite of the heavy fire from the covering force in a strongly defended position, Lieutenant Crowe and his platoon successfully attacked the posi-

tion killing 15 enemy soldiers, capturing three, and forcing the withdrawal of the remainder of the enemy. During this action Lieutenant Crowe, with complete disregard for his life, constantly exposed himself to strong enemy fire. Having cleared the enemy strong point without loss to themselves, Lieutenant Crowe and his platoon continued on their assigned mission."

Following up on that citation triggered research that turned up two big surprises.

First, I discovered I had grown up with a totally inaccurate concept of the course of Max's war. When I first started writing about Max, I believed he had fought the war almost from the beginning. But now I know he didn't hear shots fired by the Germans until late 1944, six months before the war ended.

I've been a devoted reader of military history since taking first year ROTC at the University of Wyoming. Over the years I believed that whenever I was reading about the exploits of the famed U.S. 1st Infantry Division in WW2—from its landing in North Africa in 1942 until its contact with the Russians at the Elbe in 1945—I was reading about my father.

That was because Max, who led a reconnaissance platoon, told stories about reporting recon intelligence to Major General Terry de la Mesa Allen. Allen led the 1st Infantry Division ashore in the invasion of North Africa in November, 1942 and the invasion of Sicily six months later. Max talked about serving with Allen. He seemed knowledgeable about both campaigns as well.

However, Max never fought with the 1st Infantry Division. He served only in the 104th. And he spent most of the war in Oregon training with that division.

An historical fact smokescreens this issue. Allen was the only U.S. general in WW2 who commanded two different infantry divisions. After commanding the 1st Division in North Africa and Sicily early in the war, Allen was sent home for a rest. He then took command of the 104th in Oregon on October 15, 1943 and directed its final months of training. In August, 1944 the division landed in Europe and Allen lead it from Holland to the Elbe.

So Max did serve under Allen, but not from the war's beginning to end, as I had believed for much of my life.

5 *Max Writes Home*

We'll pause here to celebrate one of the most memorable artifacts of Max's war from the family album. Max, while fighting in Holland, wrote a letter home.

Nov. 3, 1944
Holland

Dear Mother and Dad,

    I haven't found time to write for some time now. We've been pretty busy. I was in Belgium for a while and I'm now in Holland. I'm in combat and its fun to knock the Germans around. I'm getting to see a lot of foreign countries. Holland has its wooden shoes, dykes and windmills just like you hear about. I like Belgium better than any country outside of the U.S. It is more like home. It has its dances, night clubs, bars and all. I had a short visit to Paris. Boy its sure some town. I got a letter from Adalynn yesterday. She said they were all fine. I'll bet those kids are sure growing up. I got 2 letters from Donnie. I sure enjoyed them. I would sure like to be there to eat some of your good food. I'm getting plenty to eat and keeping warm. Please don't worry about me.

Love, Your Son
Max

6   *Max Supports the Canadians*

Max's October 29, 1944 bronze star citation brought a second unexpected surprise. As I read the citation I realized I was already familiar with the event it described. I knew about the attack on that German roadblock from my reading years before; even though at the time I had no idea my father might be the officer leading it, or that he had fought in that battle, or even that he had served in the 104th.

In a book about the Canadian Army, an observer described the destruction of a strong German roadblock on the first morning of the Allied advance into Holland.

As a reader I always took special interest in recon actions because my father had been a reconnaissance officer. That's why the citation later stirred buried memories from the book.

Here's the Canadian version of the story.

The senior Canadian commander was irritated with the Americans. He had been tasked with spearheading a major Allied offensive all the way from the Belgian/Dutch border to the Maas River. Even though heavy German resistance was expected, the supporting American commander had assigned green troops, the U.S. 104th Infantry Division, to cover the Canadian right flank. The 104th had arrived in Europe only two months previously and had never been tested in combat.

As I continued reading, the author reported that early in the advance the Canadian right was held up by a strong German roadblock. As the Canadians were organizing an attack, a reconnaissance unit from the neighboring American division rolled up in their armored scout cars, wiped out the roadblock, and charged on down the highway into occupied Holland.

I can't be certain that was my father. But the location and date of the action described on Max's citation agree with the beginning of the Canadian offensive. And every detail in the citation is consistent with details I remember from reading in the Canadian history, including the closing statements of both. The citation says Max's platoon, "continued on their assigned mission." The author of the Canadian account was impressed that the Americans charged in, smashed through a major German emplacement, then kept rolling toward their next objective.

As a footnote, the citation confirms that Max earned a decoration for heroism on his initial day of combat in WW2. If the two reports do recall the same action, he won that decoration during his opening minutes of combat.

The U.S. 104th Infantry Division may have been inexperienced, but it was thoroughly trained. Despite Canadian misgivings, the 104th distinguished itself on that first day of fighting at the Dutch border. And when, after almost 200 consecutive days of action against the Germans, it made contact with Russian troops at the Elbe, it had earned a reputation as one of the best U.S. infantry divisions in Europe.

✦ ✦ ✦

7 *Max Awarded Second Bronze Star*

1st Lt. Max Crowe, from Riverton, won his second Bronze Star on March 25, 1945 in Germany. He was awarded one of his Purple Hearts that day as well.

By that point in the war on the western front, the Germans were disorganized and retreating toward Berlin, hard pressed by the Allied forces. Often the only defense they could muster was a sacrificial tank or self-propelled gun left behind to delay the advancing U.S. troops. That was likely the context of Max's heroism that day.

> BRONZE STAR MEDAL CITATION
> ". . . While acting as an advance guard for a task force, Lieutenant Crowe's platoon was attacked by an enemy self-propelled gun. At great risk to his life, Lieutenant Crowe led a small patrol to the vicinity of the gun, hurling a grenade at the gun, which killed one enemy soldier and forced the others to withdraw. Lieutenant Crowe then destroyed the gun with a thermite grenade . . ."

8 The Germans Capture Max

Three days after he won his second Bronze Star, 1st Lt. Max Crowe, of Riverton, Wyoming, was taken prisoner by the Germans. Decades later, following Max's death in 1991, his wife Norma received a handwritten letter of condolence from Tom Jones, who served under Max as a sergeant.

The letter contained a rare kind of historical arti-fact, a first person account of a combat event in another soldier's life. Sargent Jones reports he watched the Germans capture Max. Here's that event extracted from the letter:

4 – 21 – 91

Dear Norma,

I am so very sorry to hear Max passed away . . .

He was my platoon leader from Oregon 1942 to Germany 1945. I was with him when he was captured. I fired [a] machine gun over his head and the Germans, but they took him into the woods and escaped. We sent a patrol around to try and recapture him and the others, but it was too late. . . .

So Max was captured on March 28, 1945, then reported missing in action. From that point onward the documented story line of Max's WW2 service gets complicated.

DON M RICKS

9 Gen. Allen Tries to Find Max

The family scrapbook contains a faded, barely legible copy of a letter typed in U.S. Army style and format. Max said it was his most treasured memento of WW2. The letter is signed by Maj. Gen. Terry de la Mesa Allen, Max's division commander.

> 21 May 1945
>
> SUBECT: Assignment of Lt Max U. Crow, [illegible serial number]
> TO: Whom it may concern.
> 1. It is urgently requested that Lt. MAX U. CROWE be re-assigned to the 104th Infantry Division with the least practicable delay prior to the re-deployment of this division to combat.
> 2. Lt Crowe has served in the reconnaissance Troop of this division since July 1943. He has had an outstanding combat record and is a distinct asset to his unit.
> [signed]
> TERRY ALLEN
> MAJOR GENERAL, COMMANDING

The urgency and high praise of the letter speak well of Max. No wonder it was special to him long after the war ended.

Seventy-five years later the letter still poses two questions. Was General Allen personally acquainted with Max, one of hundreds of junior officers in the 104th division? And for what purpose did General Allen write such a complimentary letter?

166

As to the first question, it's very likely Max did meet Allen face to face, and more than once. Allen is reputed to be the best division commander the U.S. Army had in WW2. He seemed born to that level of combat leadership. And he was a general who led from the front. So Allen likely consulted in person and frequently with the young officers who commanded the reconnaissance platoons probing ahead of the division as it advanced across Germany.

As to why Allen wrote the letter, the answer remains elusive. On first reading, the letter seems to be a straightforward personnel assignment request, though unusually imperative in tone. We know Max had been captured by the Germans on March 28th. After he had been reported missing in action for five days, his name would have been removed from the divisional roster. To get him back in the division, therefore, Allen would have to request he officially be reassigned.

As to the urgent tone of the letter, even major generals commanding have to shout sometimes to get the attention of the military bureaucrats.

That explanation unravels, however, when we look at the date of the letter: 21 May 1945. Allen's letter was written two weeks after the war ended. On April 25th a patrol from the 14th Recon Squadron was among the first units to make contact with the

Russians at the Elbe. Shortly afterward the whole U.S. advance had hooked up with the Russians. And on May 7th General Alfred Jodl unconditionally surrendered all German forces.

So when Allen wrote the May 21st letter asking for Max's reassignment to his division, the "redeployment to combat" claim was a blatant exaggeration. Allen knew the fighting was over. By then he was waiting to find out when and how his division would return to the U.S. (It departed Europe on July 3rd.)

Only one explanation of Allen's intent seems to make sense . . . Allen was assuming that Max (if still alive) had likely been liberated from a POW camp during the allied advance, and that he had disappeared among the three million U.S. Army personnel in Europe. Max, no longer belonging to a division, might be sitting in a replacement depot somewhere waiting for reassignment. Perhaps Allen hoped the letter would trigger a personnel search and return Max to the 104th so he could go home with the rest of his division. But that is just speculation on my part.

Regardless, Allen's effort was wasted, and for a reason he never would have guessed. According to a newspaper clipping in the family scrapbook, on the day Allen signed the request that Max be restored to the 104th division in Germany, Max was already back in Riverton, Wyoming, in the process of being discharged. I didn't discover that until I returned to my research after a two year pause.

10   *A story about looking for a story*

Having come up with a reasonable, if speculative, explanation for Allen's letter, I found myself at a dead end. I wanted to wrap up Max's war stories, and there were still clippings in the scrapbook. But they provided only what seemed to be routine information about his return to Wyoming.

I needed to find a story. I was not writing the history of Max's war, but a collection of stand-alone narratives. I wanted a more resonant closing than "he came home and was discharged."

I procrastinated for couple of years while writing more memoirs about growing up in Wyoming, then writing additional memoirs about what happened after I left Wyoming. Eventually I returned to the family scrapbook in case I'd overlooked something significant.

My grandfather's obituary from The Riverton Review was among the clippings. It contained a poignant mention of Max:

Schuyler Colfax Crowe, 75 years old, died Sunday

at the Bishop Randal hospital in Lander . . . His death followed by only a few days word from the War Department stating that his son, 1ˢᵗ Lt. Max U. Crowe, of an infantry reconnaissance squadron, had been reporting missing in action in Germany since March 28.

Another clipping from The Riverton Review (undated, unfortunately) reports on an interview with Max when he returned after the war:

Lt. Max U. Crow [sic], who was reported missing in action in Germany, but in reality was a prisoner of war, returned home last Friday to visit his mother, Mrs. Martha Crow, and others of his family for a short time before being sent to an army hospital in California where he will undergo a knee operation necessitated by a battle wound.

Lt. Crow has unusual experiences to tell about, for after 21 days as a prisoner of Germany he escaped and after many experiences was able to reach allied hands.

I had read that clipping earlier and remembered it contained routine facts—as well as assurance that Max had had "many unusual experiences" after escaping from the POW camp. (I knew Max's POW escape story. It was a favorite he told often over the years.)

But there was nothing there to build a story on.

Earlier I hadn't noticed, though, that the clipping continued on another column. The second part of the article had come from a different source and clearly had been written by a different (and better) writer. Here's an extract:

News that 1st Lt. Max U. Crow [sic] of Riverton has been released from a German prison camp was contained in a news release sent from France where he with other prisoners recently passed through a Recovered Allied Military Personal camp near a French port on their way home.

Hot damn. I was on the trail of a story.

11   *Max Beats the Crowd Home to Wyoming*

The story printed in The Riverton Review continued:

The Army news release, sent directly to The Review from the French port, included the names of eleven other Wyoming men . . . Each has received any necessary medical care, food, new uniforms and been given an opportunity to purchase souvenirs.

The date of the press release is missing too, unfortunately. But the release gives a distinct impression of having been written as the war was winding down, though likely not yet over. Rear echelon personnel seemed to be trying to get their troop recovery program up and running—including a public information campaign—before every American solider remaining in Europe was clamoring to be sent home.

The army press release led to two new sources. One was a copy of the Army's official plans for repatriating POWs from Europe when the war ended. The other source was a video, filmed many years after the war, in which another soldier from the 104th division told a story similar to Max's.

12   *Hyram Davidson Enters Max's story*

The video was recorded as part of an oral history series by a man named Hyram Davidson. Hyram, like Max, was a raconteur. Like Max, Hyram served with the 104th division. The Germans captured Hyram three days after they captured Max. Like Max, Hyram was sent to an embarkation camp, then arrived back in the U.S. ahead of the crowd (possibly on the same ship). Like Max, Hyrum told an adventurous tale of escaping from the POW camp. The escape story Max told probably was not true, and Hyrum's likely wasn't either.

If the closing adventure in a novel is not the most dramatic event of the book, the writer has to come up with a new ending. Perhaps that was a dilemma both raconteurs faced later when they told people how the war wrapped up for them. Watching an American tank knock down the gates of a POW camp, then walking out with the rest of the prisoners would have been a happy event. But it wouldn't have made much of a story later, back home.

(https://www.youtube.com/watch?v=Zta7AKLGkVg₊

Incidentally, Hyram's video illustrates how both he and Max, like all raconteurs who "improve" their stories, can be vulnerable to exposure by the calendar. Max said Gen. Allen's letter succeeded in getting him reassigned to the 104th division and they continued the war together. But the war had already been over for two weeks on the date Allen requested his reassignment.

Hyram spiced the story of his capture by the Germans. He recounts being captured on Easter Sunday, 1944, and adds an ironic twist. He said the Germans got him on April Fools Day. But in 1944 Easter fell on April 9th.

But those are quibbles over details. A major documented source turned up as well.

13 *Discovering the RAMP Camps*

The Army press release quoted in The Riverton Review piece said Max and 11 other soldiers from Wyoming "recently passed through a Recovered Allied Military Personnel embarkation camp."

A Google search turned up a lengthy document entitled, Administrative Repatriation Procedures & Evacuation and Disposition of Recovered Allied Military Personnel. The manual had been written late in the war, then republished (without a date, but in 2016 or later) by the recently created WW2 U.S. Medical Research Centre.

The title of the manual was: Supreme Headquarters Allied Expeditionary Force, APO 757, published Administrative Memorandum Number 48, dated 26 February 1945 governing Hospitalization and Evacuation of Recovered Allied Military Personnel.

At this point, the story of Max in WW2 again becomes in two versions. One is the version Max told that reporter in Riverton in 1945, then was still repeating to me and others 40 years later. That version included an escape from a POW camp, followed by an adventuresome odyssey back to U.S. lines. Hyrum told a similar escape story.

However, the Evacuation of Recovered Allied Military Personnel document supports a different, and certainly less dramatic, version of how both men's incarceration ended.

◆ ◆ ◆

14   *Were Max and Hyram RAMPs or MPEFETs?*

For our purposes, the crux of the matter is this: in the closing weeks of WW2 in Europe, would Lt. Max Crowe and Sergeant Hyram Davidson have been called RAMPs? Or were they considered MPEFETs?

The bureaucratic distinctions would have been little known at the time. The regulations defining them were publish only recently, and to limited distribution.

However, RAMPs vs MPEFETs reflects two entirely different realities that were playing out along the front lines as thousands of American POWs were reconnecting with U.S. forces. Some soldiers, individually or in small groups, were escaping German POW camps and finding their way back to Allied lines. Others were being liberated in large groups as the front lines overran their POW camps.

Evacuation of Recovered Allied Military Personnel declared the soldiers who were liberated by advancing units to be RAMPS (Recovered Allied Military

Personnel). The document declared those who got away on their own to be MPEFETs, or Military Personnel Escaped from Enemy Territory.

By April 1945, when Max and Hyram departed their respective POW camps (or, perhaps, the same camp) RAMP Teams were following close behind the advancing U.S. forces. They took charge of released prisoners, put them on C47s, and flew them to RAMP Camps, nineteen of which had been readied at ports along the French coast. RAMPs were fed and doctored, cleaned up, given new uniforms, and sent home on the next ship.

MPEFETs, the prisoners who escaped on their own, faced more uncertainty, including a real possibility of being shot while trying to hookup with advancing forces. Once safely inside U.S. lines, they were likely passed up the chain of headquarters until someone contacted the Military Police. The MPs, according to the procedures in place, were supposed to turn escaped prisoners over to the Military Intelligence people for debriefing.

A dozen different scenarios might have occurred for recent POWs amidst the flux of war. But only one was a sure fire route directly to a repatriation camp on the French coast, then home. That was to be among a group of POWs who were freed by advancing forces, then handed over to a RAMP Team.

We have convincing evidence that Max and Hyram were Ramps. In the video Hyram even declared himself a RAMP. He says he was sent to Camp Lucky Strike near Le Havre, the Army's biggest RAMP Camp. And the Army press release informed The Riverton Review that Max and 11 other soldiers from Wyoming had passed through a RAMP Camp.

After the war, however, Max and Hyram both told how they escaped from a POW camp, then adventuresomely reconnected with Allied forces. We can understand why. Escaping makes a much better story, obviously. Besides, what raconteur wants to spend the rest of his life looking people in the eye and saying, "When the war ended I was a MPEFET?"

We must not forget though. Max and Hyrum were much more than interesting, personable men who told good, if sometimes enhanced, war stories. Each was a sure enough hero. They both helped win World War Two.

Max and Hyrum are dead now. How I wish I could ask them one question: "Hey, did you guys ever run into each other?"

(A relevant link: www.nationalww2museum.org › camp-lucky-strike)

15 Max Sends Home Souvenirs

As to the report in The Riverton Review about soldiers getting "the opportunity to purchase souvenirs" at the repatriation camp in France, what a rear echelon wheeler-dealer operation that must have been. But Max would not have been interested. He'd already shipped home an extraordinary collection of war souvenirs.

I was about 10 when he came back. I remember the usual stuff: a Luger, Nazi award daggers, military decorations. But in addition . . . please call up some pictures stored in your mind, images of the castles of ancient German noble families. The stone walls are festooned with medieval artifacts—swords and daggers, spears and halberds, wheellock muskets, armor, those sorts of treasures.

Max led a reconnaissance platoon. The recon troops, roaming out ahead of the army, got first dibs on the good stuff. The platoon leader got firstest dibs.

August Ends

I stopped for a final look out over Phelps Lake and Jackson Hole to where my home mountains, the Wind Rivers, outlined the horizon. Then I headed Spud down the Death Canyon Trail for the last time. Sandy turned to follow, his panniers almost empty. August was ending and so was my summer as a backcountry patrol ranger in Grand Teton, my best job ever.

I watched the horse trailer pull away from the White Grass Ranger Station hauling Spud and Sandy, then drove to the warehouse to turn in my saddle and other park gear. I didn't know I would see the Grand Tetons only four more times during my lifetime, and then only during short stops, just passing through. I didn't know that, except for family visits and class reunions, I was about to leave Wyoming forever.

The story of a boy growing up in Wyoming in the 40s and 50s came to a close that day in 1959 as I drove away from park headquarters. Three weeks later I celebrated my twenty-second birthday in England at the University of Bristol where I did my first year of graduate study.

As a man who came of age in Wyoming then moved away, I played different roles over the decades in various places in the world. Today I'm an octogenarian living on a small tropical island far from town, off the grid and a dozen steps from the ocean. A few years ago I began to resurrect my Wyoming roots and started writing about my memories.

Now a new collection of stories is taking shape. I call them memories from the years of different places.

Family Photos

Cousin Jim Ridgeway, left, and Don, 8 and 9, the summer they free ranged on the farm.

Four of the Crowe brothers, Max (my father), Wayne, Jimmy, and Glynne. I've been told that Jimmy ran away from home at 14 and was never heard from again.

"You're cheating." About 1920, Riverton. Wayne and Glynn Crowe, two of my uncles, play to the camera.

Great-grandmother Simpson. All her life she grew food.

My mother, Rhoda Parker, and her sister Betty in Sheridan, presumably 1924.

From the left, my father Max Crowe (about 18) and mother Rhoda Parker (about 15). Aunt Eleanor and her boyfriend. Mom always appeared older than she was, an advantageous trait she passed to me.

1936, Max and Donnie

My uncle, Garth Crowe, in the 1930s. A note on the photo identifies him as "camp tender at Oregon Buttes pole camp" in the South Pass area. I remember him only as a dark shadow of sadness that passed between my paternal grandparents when his name was spoken. On April 1, 1940, Garth, age 31, was shot dead in Eden, Wyoming. Over the years a legend grew in the family that a jealous husband had pulled the trigger. Some of us were deeply disappointed when newspaper clippings turned up recently that said his employer shot him. The issue was a dispute over a $15.00 loan.

Don with his grandparents Martha and Schuyler Colfax Crowe and his uncle, Glynne Crowe, in Riverton in the early 40s. They farmed a small plot just southwest of town. The sewage disposal plant is located there now.

Jim Ridgeway, 1938–1958

My father, Max Crowe, is the rider nearest the camera. In 1940 he and some buddies decided it would be fun to sign a one-year enlistment in the Wyoming National Guard and ride the horses together. He was discharged five years later, having been commissioned, wounded, decorated for valor, and captured by the Germans as the war was winding down.

Acknowledgements

Barbara Lockwood, for making the whole project happen.
Julie Morgan, for her superb cover design.
Michael Copini, who kept a computer illiterate online all these years.
Margaret Herriman, granddaughter, for honest advice and editorial suggestions.
Dwain Romsa for allowing me to stretch the rules.
Jane Botkin for the support only a fellow writer can provide.
Mike Anderson, Tom Davis, Clint Black, and Jack Hallam for being there, post after post, year after year. Kay Jessen for good marketing suggestions.
For likes, comments, and encouragement over the years:
Kristin Quevedo,
Larry Jones, Gary Vickrey, Debi Moody, Patsy bixby Parkin, Holly Anderson Smothers, Bill Sanders, Roger Kahn, Linda Kobel Moench, Len Sostrum, Tracy Hulston, Dave Smith, Jack Shinkle, Dave Rupp, Matthew Hutson, Gretchen Pili, Leone Maier Hay, David Frahm, Barbara Hakes, Bruce Deuel, Donna Even, Justin Flansburg, Marge Carmichael, Jery R Walters, Jackson N Renee Stewart, Loren Hunt, Jorge Echeverria, Joel Gomez, Dave King, Larry Rohrbacher, Ob Lyon, Caroline Applehans, Francine Ward Weliver, Melinda Ambrose, Jodi Moll, Mike Neumann, Melissa Brownell, Gail Allison Leslie, Ron Patterson, Diane Debroski Wolski, Glenn Lewis, Barbara Kolar Bergstrom, Susan Riggs, and the scores of others I forgot to mention.

Cover photo: "Donnie," late 1930's, at the Crowe family farm near Riverton where the sewage disposal plant is now located.
Photo rights: Don M Ricks

ABOUT THE AUTHOR

Don M Ricks

Don M. Ricks, now 85, was lured into higher education by a Wyoming Cowboys football scholarship. Ten years and four universities later he was handed another degree and told to find work. Whatever his job since, in academia or business, he's primarily been a writer. He published a book club selection so long ago no one cares and more articles and learning texts than anyone remembers. When the invention of desktop publishing created new life opportunities, he and Barbara bought a 50-foot sailboat and went south. Now living off the grid and near the water in the Caribbean, they write for Bonaire's English language newspaper. True to his Wyoming roots, Don raised his kids on a ranch in the foothills while commuting to Calgary.

Made in United States
Orlando, FL
01 April 2022

16391111R00111